D1234060

Federal Rules of Evidence
with Objections

DAN KROCKER
ATTORNEY AT LAW
710 NORTH POST OAK RD # 400
HOUSTON TX 77024
(713) 683-0397

Federal Rules of Evidence with Objections

Reflects changes made to the Federal Rules of Evidence through December 1, 2006

Seventh Edition

Anthony J. Bocchino
Jack E. Feinberg Professor of Litigation
Temple University Beasley School of Law

David A. Sonenshein
I. Herman Stern Professor of Law
Temple University Beasley School of Law

National Institute for Trial Advocacy

Reproduction Permission
National Institute for Trial Advocacy
361 Centennial Parkway, Suite 220
Louisville, CO 80027
(800) 225-6482   Fax (720) 890-7069
Web site: www.nita.org

© 1992, 1993, 1994, 1995, 1997, 1998, 2000, 2003, 2006
by the National Institute for Trial Advocacy
Printed in the United States of America. All rights reserved.

Bocchino, Anthony J., and David A. Sonenshein,
Federal Rules of Evidence with Objections, Seventh Edition,
(First Edition, 1992).

ISBN-10: 1-60156-013-3
ISBN-13: 978-1-60156-013-1
August 2006 printing.

Library of Congress Cataloging-in-Publication Data

Cataloging-in-Publication data is available from the Library of Congress.

Table of Contents

Federal Rules of Evidence with Objections

Federal Rules of Evidence with Objections

Impeachment

Federal Rules of Evidence with Objections

Preface

The following text is designed to provide the practitioner and student with a convenient reference for raising trial objections and presenting responses. This pocket-sized reference book affords the user the opportunity to instantly consult the relevant section of the Federal Rules of Evidence which are reproduced in their entirety in the last section of the book.

The material is presented in alphabetical order; tabs are located on the edges of the pages to aid in locating the appropriate section. Responses are found on the same pages/sections as the objections.

The cross reference to the applicable Federal Rule(s) follows the objections and responses and an "Explanation" paragraph concludes each topic. This explanatory segment is designed to alert the reader to a practice tip or legal interpretation crucial to proper understanding of the subject matter of that section.

This book is not designed to provide an in-depth analysis of evidentiary rulings or the application of the theories concerning the admission or exclusion of evidence. Instead, *Federal Rules of Evidence with Objections* was developed to furnish users with a complete reference of trial objections and responses, and is small enough to be easily carried to the courtroom or the classroom. We hope you find this material assists you in the pursuit of improving your litigation skills.

National Institute for Trial Advocacy

Ambiguous Questions

Objection

- *I object that the question is* (ambiguous—vague—unintelligible).

Response

In most circumstances it is better to rephrase the question unless counsel is certain of the question's clarity.

Cross Reference to Federal Rule

[There is no federal rule specifically covering forms of questions. The court has discretion to sustain the objection pursuant to Rule 611(a).]

Explanation

An ambiguous question is one that is susceptible to at least two interpretations, or that is so vague or unintelligible as to make it likely to confuse the jury or witness.

Argumentative Questions

Objections

- *I object. The question is argumentative.*
- *I object. Counsel is arguing to the jury.*

Response

- *I am trying to elicit evidence from the witness.*

Cross Reference to Federal Rule

[There is no federal rule specifically covering forms of questions. The court has discretion to sustain the objection pursuant to Rule 611(a).]

Explanation

An argumentative question is one which does not seek information from the witness but rather makes an argument to the jury in the guise of a question.

The objection to an argumentative question is not intended to cover the situation where the questioning counsel is arguing with the witness; rather, it applies to the situation where counsel comments on the evidence or attempts to draw inferences from the evidence thereby seeking the witness's response to such comments. It is jury argument in the guise of a question.

Asked and Answered Questions

Objections

- *I object. The question has been asked and answered.*

- *I object. The witness has already answered that question.*

Responses

- *The witness has not yet answered the question.*

- *The question has not been answered during my examination.*

Cross Reference to Federal Rule

[There is no federal rule specifically covering forms of questions. The court has discretion to sustain the objection pursuant to Rule 611(a). The objection may be sustained, however, pursuant to Rule 403.]

Explanation

A question may be objected to as "asked and answered" when it calls for the repetition of testimony from a witness who has previously given the same testimony in response to a question asked by examining counsel. It is designed to prevent cumulative evidence through repetition of testimony.

Assuming Facts Not in Evidence

Objection

- *I object. The question assumes a fact not in evidence. There has been no testimony that* (insert facts that have been assumed).

Responses

- *I will elicit that fact from the witness in a separate question.*

- *That fact has been proved during the earlier testimony of this witness.*

- *That fact has been proved during the testimony of* (insert the name of another witness who has already testified).

- *This fact will be testified to during the testimony of* (insert the name of another witness who will testify later).

Cross Reference to Federal Rule

[There is no federal rule specifically covering forms of questions. The court has discretion to sustain the objection pursuant to Rule 611(a).]

Explanation

A question is objectionable if it assumes, in the asking, facts that have not already been proved. These questions are another form of leading questions, and are referred to as "misleading" questions.

Authentication of Instruments

Objection

- *I object. This exhibit has not been authenticated.*

Responses

- *This instrument has been authenticated by stipulation of counsel.*

- *The instrument has been authenticated through the testimony of* (insert name of witness) *who has testified that:*

  - *the witness created the writing,* or

  - *the witness was present when the writing was created and testified that it is in substantially the same condition as at the time of its creation,* or

  - *the witness knows the handwriting because (s)he saw the author write or sign the instrument,* or

  - *the witness knows the handwriting from having seen the author sign at another time,* or

  - *the witness knows the handwriting by circumstantial evidence* (state such circumstantial evidence), or

  - (where document is proved by an expert witness) *the expert has compared the handwriting in question with an authentic handwriting exemplar and that the expert's opinion to a reasonable degree of certainty is that the handwriting in question is that of* (insert name of purported author), or

- *the witness was present at the time the tape recording, audio, or video, was made,* or

- *the witness saw the scene or items portrayed in the photograph at a relevant time and that the photograph is a fair and accurate representation of what was seen.*

- *I request the court compare the handwriting in question with an admittedly authentic handwriting exemplar and find that it is the handwriting of* (insert name of purported author).

Cross Reference to Federal Rule 901

Explanation

Before an instrument can be admitted in evidence, the proponent must establish its identity by stipulation, circumstantial evidence, the testimony of a witness with knowledge of its identity and authorship, or self-authenication or certification pursuant to Rule 902.

Authentication of Telephone Conversation and Voices

Objections

- *I object. The telephone conversation has not been authenticated.*

- *I object. The participants in the telephone conversation have not been properly identified.*

Responses

- *The identity of the participants in the telephone conversation has been established through the testimony of* (insert name of witness) *who has testified that:*

  - *the witness is familiar with and recognized the voice,* or

  - *the witness called the number listed to* (insert name of participant) *and the other party identified himself or herself as* (insert name of participant), or

  - *the witness called the number listed to* (insert name of participant) *and the content of the conversation showed* (insert name of person) *to be the person who answered the call,* or

  - *the witness called the number listed to* (insert name of business) *and the conversation related to business conducted by* (insert name of business) *over the telephone,* or

- (where proof is established by expert witness testimony) *the expert has compared the voice in question with an authentic voice exemplar and that the expert's opinion to a reasonable degree of certainty is that the voice in question is that of* (insert name of purported speaker).

Cross Reference to Federal Rule 901

Explanation

Authentication of telephone conversations and voices is the process of proving the identity of the persons involved in the conversation. Before testimony can be had that a telephone conversation occurred, testimony must be elicited to prove the identity of the participants in the conversation.

Character Evidence: Generally

Objection

- *The question calls for (or the answer provides) evidence of character offered on propensity.*

Response

- *This evidence is:*
  - *offered on propensity pursuant to Rule 404(a)(1) or 404(a)(2), or*
  - *offered for a relevant, non-propensity purpose under Rule 404(b), or*
  - *offered to prove propensity where character is an essential element of a claim, charge, or defense under Rule 405(b).*

Cross Reference to Federal Rules 404 and 405

Explanation

The evidence of a person's character is generally inadmissible as irrelevant when offered on the issue of that person's propensity to act in conformity with such character trait. When a criminal defendant puts in issue his or her own character, or the character of the alleged victim, or where the character of a party is an essential element of a claim, charge, or defense in either the criminal or civil context, character evidence is admissible to show propensity.

Character Evidence: Accused or Victim in a Criminal Case

Objections

- *I object. The prosecution is attempting to offer evidence of the defendant's character where the defendant has not offered any character evidence.*

- *I object. The prosecution is attempting to offer evidence of the victim's character where none has been offered by the defendant.*

Responses

- *The defendant has opened the door on his or her character by offering evidence of his or her pertinent character trait.*

- *The defendant has opened the door on the victim's character by:*
  - *offering evidence of the victim's character,* or
  - *offering evidence that the victim was the first aggressor in a homicide case.*

Cross Reference to Federal Rules 404 and 405

Explanation

Where the accused in a criminal case opens the door to his or her own good character pursuant to Rule 404(a)(1) or to the victim's character pursuant to Rule 404(a)(2), then the prosecution is permitted to rebut that evidence with contrary character evidence. Rule 404(a)(1) permits a criminal defendant to offer reputation or opinion evidence, through a character witness, to show lack of propensity to commit the crime charged. Rule 404(a)(2) allows the criminal defendant to offer evidence of the victim's relevant character trait to show the propensity of the victim to act in a certain way where pertinent. Note that after the criminal defendant offers bad character evidence of the victim pursuant to Rule 404(a)(2), the government may offer bad character evidence of the defendant on the same trait whether or not the defendant offered good character evidence of himself. Rule 404(a)(1) and Rule 404(a)(2) character evidence may only be proved by reputation or opinion evidence. If the character of the defendant is an essential element of the charge or defense, that character may be proved by specific instances of conduct by the defendant in addition to by way of reputation and opinion evidence.

Character Evidence:
Other Acts, Crimes, or Wrongs

Objection

- *I object. This evidence is inadmissible character evidence offered on propensity.*

Response

- *This evidence is not offered on propensity, but rather for the purpose of showing* (state purpose), *a relevant, non-propensity purpose, pursuant to Rule 404(b).*

Cross Reference to Federal Rule 404(b)

Explanation

Rule 404(b) is not an exception to the general rule forbidding the use of character evidence to show propensity. Rather, Rule 404(b) admits character evidence where it involves specific crimes, wrongs, or acts, other than those involved in the case at bar, for any relevant, non-propensity purpose, including the commonly enumerated purposes illustrated in the rule. Assuming that the prior act is otherwise admissible, the quantum of proof necessary for its admission must meet the Rule 104 standard of sufficient evidence that the jury could find that the specific instance of conduct occurred. In a criminal case, the prosecution must give reasonable notice as to any evidence that it intends to offer pursuant to Rule 404(b).

Character Evidence:
Prior Sexual Activity
of Alleged Victim
(The Rape Shield)

Objections

Civil Cases

- (Opinion evidence) *I object. The question calls for opinion evidence concerning the sexual behavior or sexual predisposition of a victim of sexual misconduct.*

- (Reputation evidence) *I object. The question calls for reputation evidence concerning sexual behavior or sexual predisposition of a victim of sexual misconduct and the victim has not placed his/her reputation in issue.*

- (Specific instances of conduct) *I object. The question calls for evidence concerning the sexual behavior or sexual predisposition of a victim of sexual misconduct and it is irrelevant.*

Criminal Cases

- (Opinion or reputation evidence) *I object. The question calls for opinion or reputation evidence concerning the victim's sexual behavior or sexual predisposition.*

- (Specific instances of conduct) *I object. The question calls for evidence concerning the issue of the victim's sexual conduct or sexual predisposition and is irrelevant.*

Responses

Civil Cases

- (Opinion evidence) There is no appropriate response.

- (Reputation evidence) *The victim of sexual misconduct put his/her reputation for sexual behavior or sexual predisposition in issue when the following evidence was offered* (insert evidence that opened the door to sexual repuation evidence).

- (Specific instances of conduct) *The evidence of sexual behavior or sexual predisposition is otherwise admissible under Federal Rules of Evidence 404 or 405 and the probative value of the evidence substantially outweighs the harm to the victim of sexual misconduct, or the unfair prejudice to any party.*

Criminal Cases

- (Opinion or reputation evidence) There is no appropriate response.

- (Specific instances of conduct) *The evidence of sexual behavior is admissible:*

  (a) to prove that someone other than the defendant was the source of semen, injury or other physical evidence;

  (b) as it was with the defendant and offered by the defendant to prove the consent of the victim;

  (c) as it is offered by the prosecution; or

  (d) as it is offered by the defendant and the failure to admit the evidence of sexual behavior or sexual predisposition would violate the consitutional rights of the defendant

  and

  proper notice has been given to the victim and the parties and the judge has determined, in camera, that the evidence is admissible.

Cross Reference to Federal Rules 412, 404, and 405

Explanation

This 1994 amendment to Rule 412 makes a distinction between civil and criminal cases. In a civil case, opinion evidence concerning sexual behavior or sexual predisposition of the victim of sexual misconduct is never admissible, while reputation evidence concerning the very same character matters may be admissible if it is first raised by the victim. In civil cases, specific instances of conduct offered to prove the sexual behavior or sexual predisposition of a victim of sexual misconduct are admissible, if otherwise admissible under the rules of evidence (e.g., pursuant to Rules 404 or 405), and the judge determines that the probative value of the evidence substantially outweighs the harm to the victim or the unfair prejudice to any party.

In criminal cases opinion or reputation evidence concerning the sexual behavior or sexual predisposition of a victim of sexual misconduct is never admissible. Specific instances of conduct showing sexual behavior on the part of the victim of sexual misconduct are admissible if offered to prove that someone other than the defendant is the source of semen, physical injury, or other physical condition, or if the sexual conduct was with the defendant, and offered on the issue of consent. Evidence of specific instances of conduct on the part of the victim of sexual misconduct are admissible if they show either sexual behavior <u>or</u> sexual predisposition if the exclusion of such evidence would violate the constitutional rights of the defendant.

Character Evidence: Similar Crimes or Acts in Civil or Criminal Sexual Assault or Child Molestation Cases

Objection

- *I object that this evidence is inadmissible character evidence offered on propensity.*

Response

- *This offer involves evidence of a similar crime of sexual assault or child molestation, offered*
  - *in a criminal case charging sexual assault or child molestation, or*
  - *in a civil case concerning sexual assault or child molestation.*

Cross Reference to Federal Rules 413, 414, and 415

Explanation

Rule 404(a) generally excludes evidence of similar acts when offered to prove the propensity of the civil or criminal defendant to commit the act which is charged. New Rules 413, 414, and 415 create an exception for such offers in cases involving sexual assault or child molestation.

Of course, under Rule 403 the admission of such evidence remains subject to exclusion if it is prejudicial or confusing, or involves an undue waste of time. However, it is unavailing to argue that the evidence of similar crimes will prejudice the jury by inviting the inference that the defendant committed the crime or act alleged in the instant case because he committed a similar crime on an earlier occasion. After all, that inference is the very basis for admitting the similar crime evidence pursuant to Rules 413, 414, and 415.

Finally, note that in both civil and criminal cases, the proponent of an offer of similar acts evidence pursuant to Rules 413, 414, and 415 must disclose such evidence to the party against whom it is offered fifteen days before trial.

Compound Questions

Objection

- *I object. The question is compound.*

Response

- *I withdraw the question and will ask separate questions.*

Cross Reference to Federal Rule 611

Explanation

A compound question asks for two or more items of information at the same time, so that it is impossible to understand the meaning of the answer to the question. Objections to compound questions are best made only when the compound question is likely to mislead the jury to the detriment of objecting counsel's client. Otherwise the objection merely makes the opponent a better questioner.

Compromise/ Offers of Compromise

Objection

- *I object. The proffered evidence is evidence of compromise negotiations offered on liability and / or damages.*

Responses

- *The evidence is admissible because:*
  - *the claim was not in dispute at the time of the compromise discussions,* or
  - *the evidence is not offered on liability or damages but to show: bias, no undue delay, or an effort to subvert a criminal investigation.*

Cross Reference to Federal Rule 408

Explanation

Evidence of settlement or of settlement negotiations in a disputed civil claim are inadmissible to prove liability or the amount of the claim. Evidence of settlement, offers to settle, or statements made during the course of settlement negotiations may be admissible for another relevant purpose, e.g., to show bias, to negate allegations of undue delay, or an effort to subvert a criminal investigation or prosecution.

Cross Examination:
Generally

Objection

- *I move to strike the direct testimony of the witness because I have not had the opportunity to conduct a full and fair cross examination. I ask that the jury be instructed to disregard the testimony of the witness.*

Responses

- *The purposes of cross examination have been substantially completed.*
- *Counsel has waived the right to a full and complete cross examination by* (insert reasons).

Cross Reference to Federal Rule 611(a)

[There is no federal rule which specifically addresses the issue of the right to a full and fair cross examination.]

Explanation

As to every witness presented by a party, the adverse party has the right to a full and fair cross examination. The remedy for the denial of such right is to have the testimony stricken from the record.

Cross Examination: Scope

Objection

- *I object. The question on cross examination exceeds the scope of direct examination.*

Responses

- *The subject matter of the question was raised when the witness testified on direct examination that* (insert prior testimony).

- *The question seeks to elicit information that is relevant to the credibility of the witness.*

- *I request the court allow inquiry outside the scope of direct examination. I will conduct the inquiry of the witness as if on direct examination.*

Cross Reference to Federal Rule 611(b)

Explanation

The rule limiting cross examination to those matters on direct examination does not limit questioning on cross to the answers elicited on direct, but rather to the subject matter raised or implicated by the direct examination. It also allows inquiry into matters affecting the credibility of the witness.

A B C Cross examination that exceeds the scope of direct examination must be conducted as if it were a direct examination.

Exhibits: Demonstrative

Objections

- *I object. The proffered exhibit has not been properly authenticated.*

- *I object. The proffered exhibit has not been shown to be:*
  - (photographs) *a fair and accurate depiction of a relevant scene,* or
  - (to-scale models) *a fair and accurate representation of an object in issue.*

Responses

- *The demonstrative exhibit has been authenticated by the testimony of* (insert name of witness). *The witness has testified that:*
  - (photographs) *the exhibit looks like an object in issue,* or
  - (to-scale models) *the exhibit is a fair and accurate representation of a scene in issue.*

- (Photographs) *The witness has testified that the photograph shows a relevant scene as it appeared at a relevant time and the exhibit is a fair and accurate depiction of that scene.*

- (To-scale models) *The witness has testified that the exhibit is a to-scale model and is a fair and accurate representation of an object that is in issue.*

Cross Reference to Federal Rule

[There is no specific rule on demonstrative exhibits. All exhibits must be authenticated pursuant to Rule 901(a).]

Explanation

Typical demonstrative exhibits are photographs and to-scale models. The requirement of authentication of such exhibits is satisfied by evidence sufficient to support a finding that the exhibit is a fair and accurate depiction or representation of something that is in issue in a case.

Exhibits:
Illustrative

Objections

D
E
F

- *I object. The proffered illustrative exhibit has not been properly authenticated.*

- *I object. The proffered illustrative exhibit is confusing and / or misleading.*

- *I object. The proffered illustrative exhibit contains markings that will lead the witness in the giving of testimony.*

Responses

- *The illustrative exhibit has been authenticated by the testimony of* (insert name of witness). *The witness testified that:*

  - *the witness recognizes what the exhibit, that has been marked for identification, portrays,* and

  - *the exhibit will aid in the illustration and / or explanation of the witness's testimony.*

- *The exhibit is not offered as a to-scale diagram; it is merely an aid to the explaining of testimony. Any problems with the illustrative exhibit can be demonstrated during cross examination.*

- (Insert name of witness) *has already testified as to what the markings contained on the exhibit portray. The exhibit is offered merely to illustrate that testimony.*

D E F Cross Reference to Federal Rule

[There is no specific rule on illustrative exhibits. All exhibits must be authenticated pursuant to Rule 901(a).]

Explanation

Illustrative exhibits are those which assist a witness in the rendering of testimony. Examples of illustrative exhibits are diagrams, charts, and graphs. The requirement of authentication is satisfied as to illustrative exhibits by testimony that the exhibit will aid in the illustrating or explaining of testimony.

Exhibits:
Tangible Objects

Objection

- *I object. The proffered exhibit is incompetent for lack of proper foundation.*

Response

- *I have shown through the testimony of* (insert name of witness) *that*
  - *he or she perceived the exhibit at a relevant time,* and
  - *the exhibit is the one perceived,* and
  - *it is in substantially the same condition as it was at the relevant time.*

Cross Reference to Federal Rule

[There is no specific rule on tangible objects exhibits. All exhibits must be authenticated pursuant to Rule 901(a).]

Explanation

In order to introduce a tangible object into evidence, the proponent must show that it can be identified by a witness who had knowledge of the tangible object at a relevant time and who can testify that the tangible object is in the same or substantially the same condition as it was at a relevant time.

Expert Opinion

Objections

- *I object to the qualification of the witness as an expert.*

- *I object to the admission of expert testimony because the discipline in which the witness purports to qualify will not provide information that is helpful to jury determination or understanding of any fact in issue.*

- *I object to the admission of the witness's opinion because it is beyond the area of expertise in which he or she has been qualified.*

Responses

- *I have shown that the witness is qualified as an expert in* (insert field of expertise) *through the witness's knowledge, skill, experience, training, or education.*

- *I have shown that the area of expertise in which the witness is qualified is one that will be helpful to the jury in determining* (insert fact or conclusion in issue.)

- *The court has qualified the expert in the area of* (insert field of expertise) *and the witness's opinion is within that area.*

Cross Reference to Federal Rules 702, 703, 704, 705, and 706

Explanation

Where the proponent seeks to offer opinions, conclusions, or inferences to assist the fact-finder in determining a fact in issue, and such opinions are beyond the ability of the fact-finder, the proponent may offer such opinions, conclusions, or inferences from a witness qualified as an expert in the relevant field. The proponent of the expert opinion bears the burden of laying a foundation demonstrating the expertise of the purported expert and the reliability of the methodology, principle, or process the expert uses to reach a conclusion.

Though an expert is permitted to rely on otherwise inadmissible, but reliable, data to form the opinion, the expert may not disclose the substance of the inadmissible data to the jury unless the court finds that its probative value in assisting the jury to evaluate the expert's opinion substantially outweighs its prejudice.

Firsthand Knowledge

Objection

- *I object. There has been no foundation to show the witness has personal knowledge of the matter about which he or she has been asked.*

Response

- *The witness has shown firsthand knowledge of the subject matter of the witness's testimony. A foundation has been laid which demonstrates the witness was in position to know those items about which his or her testimony will be given.*

Cross Reference to Federal Rule 602

Explanation

A witness may testify only as to the matters about which he or she has personal or firsthand knowledge. Lack of personal knowledge makes the witness incompetent to testify as to particular facts. Generally, the proponent of the witness must lay a foundation on the issue of personal knowledge by offering evidence sufficient to support a finding that the witness had firsthand knowledge of the subject matter about which testimony will be given.

Guilty Pleas
(Offers of Pleas and Related Statements)

Objection

- *I object that this evidence is inadmissible as a withdrawn guilty plea, as a nolo contendere plea, or as an offer to so plead.*

Response

- *This evidence is admissible against the criminal defendant because the defendant is charged with perjury and the statement was made under oath, in the presence of counsel, and on the record.*

Cross Reference to Federal Rule 410

Explanation

Evidence of the plea and statements connected therewith are admissible against a criminal defendant, but only when he or she is charged with perjury or making false statements, and if the statement is on the record, and made under oath and in the presence of counsel.

Habit and Routine Practice

Objection

- *I object. This evidence is irrelevant in that it is such an isolated occurrence as to be insufficient to constitute a habit or routine practice.*

Response

- *This evidence is relevant because it shows:*
  - *a consistent habit or routine practice which raises a permissible inference that the party or organization likely acted in this case according to the habit or routine practice.*

Cross Reference to Federal Rule 406

Explanation

Evidence of a personal habit or of the routine practice of an organization is admissible as relevant to show that on a specific occasion, such person or organization acted in conformity with the proffered habit or practice. By its nature, habit or routine practice testimony is circumstantial proof that certain conduct, or an act consistent therewith, occurred. Habit or routine practice evidence is admissible even when there is firsthand evidence of the conduct in question.

Hearsay:
Generally

Objections

- *I object. The question calls for a hearsay answer.*

- *I move to strike the answer as hearsay.*

Response

- *The statement is not being offered for the truth of the matter asserted, but rather is offered to show the statement was made. The making of the statement is relevant to show:*

  - *the effect on a person who heard the statement,* or

  - *a prior inconsistent statement,* or

  - *the operative facts or a verbal act,* or

  - *the knowledge of the declarant.*

Cross Reference to Federal Rule 801

Explanation

The foolproof hearsay test: Ask the question whether the relevant purpose for offering the out-of-court statement is its truth. If the answer to that question is "yes," the out-of-court statement is hearsay. If the answer to the question is not clearly "yes," ask this next question: "Must the content of the out-of-court statement be believed in order to be relevant?" If yes, the evidence is hearsay.

Hearsay:
Attacking and Supporting the Credibility of a Hearsay Declarant

Objection

- *I object. The question seeks to attack the credibility of a person who has not appeared as a witness.*

Response

- *This impeachment of an out-of-court declarant is permissible to the same extent available for a testifying witness.*

Cross Reference to Federal Rule 806

Explanation

Impeachment of an out-of-court declarant is permissible to the same extent available for a testifying witness. Impeachment by prior inconsistent statement of a hearsay declarant is permitted despite the inability to confront the declarant with the inconsistency to afford him or her an opportunity to admit or deny, as is required by Rule 613(b). Impeachment of the hearsay declarant as to bias, interest, prejudice, or improper motive may be accomplished without the usual foundational requirement of denial of the same.

Hearsay:
Non-Hearsay Admissions

Objections

- *I object. The question calls for a hearsay answer.*

- *I move to strike the answer as hearsay.*

Responses

- *The statement is not hearsay pursuant to Rule 801(d)(2) because I have shown that:*

  - *The statement was made by the party opponent,* or

  - *The statement was made by a person and was adopted by the party opponent as the party's own, and is thus, a vicarious admission of the party opponent,* or

  - *The statement was made by an agent authorized to speak on behalf of a party opponent, and is thus, a vicarious admission of the party opponent,* or

  - *The statement was made by an agent authorized to speak on behalf of the party opponent concerning a matter within the scope of the declarant's agency or employment, and was made during the existence of the declarant's agency or employment, and thus, is a vicarious admission of a party opponent,* or

- *The statement was made by a co-conspirator of the party opponent during the course of the conspiracy and in furtherance of the conspiracy, and thus, is a vicarious admission of the party opponent.*

Cross Reference to Federal Rule 801(d)(2)

Explanation

The Federal Rules define as non-hearsay any admission of a party opponent. An admission is an out-of-court statement made by a party or attributable to a party offered for its truth by the opponent in the lawsuit. For purposes of proving the existence of a conspiracy for co-conspirator admissions, the proponent may offer the alleged co-conspirator statement itself. The content of the statement shall be considered but alone is not sufficient to establish agency or employment or scope of employment in Rule 801(d)(2)(C) or (D) or the existence of the conspiracy or the participation of the declarant or party in the conspiracy in Rule 801(d)(2)(E).

Hearsay:
Non-Hearsay Prior Statements

Objections

- *I object. The question calls for a hearsay answer.*

- *I move to strike the answer as hearsay.*

Responses

- *The statement is not hearsay pursuant to Rule 801(d)(1) because I have shown that:*

  - *it is inconsistent with the witness's trial testimony and was given under oath at an earlier proceeding or deposition, or*

  - *it is consistent with the witness's trial testimony and is offered to rebut an express or implied charge of recent fabrication, or improper influence or motive, or*

  - *the statement by the testifying witness is an identification of a person made after perceiving such person.*

Cross Reference to Federal Rule
801(d)(1)(A-C)

Explanation

Out-of-court statements made by a declarant who is testifying in trial are not hearsay: if the declarant is subject to cross examination, if the statement is inconsistent with previous trial testimony and given under oath subject to the penalty of perjury, if the statement is consistent with prior testimony and is offered for the purpose of rebutting an express or implied charge of recent fabrication or improper influence or motive, or if the statement is one of identification of a person based on perception.

G

H

Hearsay Within Hearsay

Objections

- *I object. The question calls for hearsay within hearsay.*

- *I move to strike the answer because it contains hearsay within hearsay.*

Response

- *Both statements are admissible because each either comes within a hearsay exception or is non-hearsay.*

Cross Reference to Federal Rule 805

Explanation

In order to admit hearsay within hearsay, the proponent must account for both out-of-court statements with either a hearsay exception, or an argument that the out-of-court statement is offered for a relevant, non-hearsay purpose.

Hearsay Exception: Absence of Entry in Business Records

Objections

- *I object. The question calls for hearsay.*

- *I move to strike the answer as hearsay.*

Response

- *The absence of an entry in this record is admissible to show the nonoccurrence of an event pursuant to Rule 803(7). I have shown through the testimony of* (insert name of witness) *who is the custodian of the business records, or other qualified person that:*

  - *a business record exists, pursuant to Rule 803(6),* and

  - *the matter which is not recorded in the record is of a kind for which a record would regularly be made and preserved,* and

  - *the source of the information or other circumstances fail to indicate a lack of trustworthiness.*

Cross Reference to Federal Rule 803(6), (7)

Explanation

If the proponent is able to lay a foundation for a record of regularly conducted activity pursuant to Rule 803(6), testimony or the offer of the record for the purpose of demonstrating that a particular entry does not appear in the record is permitted for the purpose of proving that the event, about which the record would have been made, did not occur.

Hearsay Exception:
Absence of Public Records
or Entry

Objections

- *I object. The question calls for a hearsay answer.*

- *I move to strike the answer as hearsay.*

Response

- *Evidence of a diligent but unavailing search of the records of the public agency or office is admissible pursuant to the hearsay exception contained in Rule 803(10). I have shown through a certification which complies with Rule 902 or through the testimony of* (insert name of witness) *that:*

  - *a public agency or office regularly makes and preserves records of a particular kind of matter,* and

  - *a diligent but unavailing search of such records failed to disclose a record, report, statement, data compilation, or entry regarding a particular alleged happening of such a matter.*

Cross Reference to Federal Rule 803(10)

Explanation

The absence of a public record or entry concerning an event that would normally be the subject of a public record is admissible to prove that the event did not occur.

Hearsay Exception: Excited Utterance

Objections

- *I object. The question calls for a hearsay answer.*
- *I move to strike the answer as hearsay.*

Responses

- *The statement is admissible as an excited utterance pursuant to Rule 803(2). I have shown through the testimony of* (insert name of witness) *that the statement:*
  - *relates to a startling event or condition,* and
  - *was made while the declarant was under the stress or excitement caused by the event or condition.*

Cross Reference to Federal Rule 803(2)

Explanation

When the declarant is sufficiently startled into making a spontaneous utterance, the assumption is there was neither sufficient time nor presence of mind to fabricate. The event which gives rise to the statement relating to it must be sufficiently startling, and the statement must be made under the stress of that event, so as to remove the likelihood of self-serving reflection in the making of the statement.

Hearsay Exception: Family Records

Objections

- *I object. The question calls for a hearsay answer.*

- *I move to strike the answer as hearsay.*

Responses

- *This statement is admissible as a family record pursuant to Rule 803(13). I have shown through the testimony of* (insert name of witness) *that this is a statement of fact:*

  - *concerning personal or family history,*

  - *contained in family Bibles, genealogies, or the like.*

Cross Reference to Federal Rule 803(13)

Explanation

Statements of personal or family history contained in volumes or in other places where, if they were inaccurate, would have been corrected, are admissible to prove the content of those statements. Note the absence of a requirement of contemporaneity of entry. However, such writing, like any other, must be authenticated.

Hearsay Exception: Forfeiture by Wrongdoing

Objections

- *I object. The question calls for hearsay.*

- *I move to strike the answer as hearsay.*

Responses

G
H

- *This statement is admissible pursuant to Rule 804(b)(6). I have shown through the testimony of* (insert the names of the witness(es)) *that:*
  - *the declarant is unavailable pursuant to Rule 804(a),*
  - *objecting counsel's client engaged in wrongdoing that was intended, and did, procure the unavailability of the declarant*
    or
  - *objecting counsel's client acquiesced in wrongdoing that was intended to, and did, procure the unavailability of the declarant.*

Cross Reference to Federal Rule 804(b)(6)

Explanation

A party forfeits the right to object on hearsay grounds to any statement made by a person whose unavailability has been procured by the wrongdoing of the party. Forfeiture also applies if the wrongful conduct that procured the unavailability of the hearsay declarant was acquiesced in by the party. The purpose of this exception is to provide a disincentive to procuring the unavailability by any wrongdoing. The exception is based on the notion that a party who procures or acquiesces in the procuring of a witness by wrongdoing, should not be allowed to benefit from that wrongdoing by disallowing the witness's previous statements on hearsay grounds.

G

H

Hearsay Exception: Former Testimony

Objections

- *I object. The question calls for a hearsay answer.*

- *I move to strike the answer as hearsay.*

Responses

- *The statement is admissible as former testimony pursuant to Rule 804(b)(1). I have shown through the testimony of* (insert name of witness) *that:*

  - *The declarant is unavailable pursuant to Rule 804(a),*

  - *the statement is testimony given*

  - *at another hearing of the same or different proceeding, or in a deposition in the course of the same or a different proceeding,* and

  - *the party against whom it is offered had an opportunity and similar motive to develop the testimony by direct, cross, or redirect examination.*

Cross Reference to Federal Rule 804

Explanation

Former testimony is any testimony given under oath in an earlier proceeding. It is admissible at a later hearing if the declarant is unavailable, and the party against whom it is now offered had the opportunity and a similar motive to develop, by questioning of the declarant, the earlier testimony when it was given. The reliability of these statements is gained from the fact that they were given under oath, and could be tested by examination by the party against whom they are now offered.

G
H

Hearsay Exception:
Judgment as to Personal, Family, or General History, or Boundaries

Objections

- *I object. The question calls for a hearsay answer.*

- *I move to strike the answer as hearsay.*

Response

- *This statement is admissible as a judgment relating to personal, family, or general history, or boundaries pursuant to Rule 803(23). I have shown through the testimony of* (insert name of witness) *that this statement is a:*

  - *judgment offered as proof of*

  - *personal, family, or general history,* or *boundaries,*

  - *essential to the judgment,* and

  - *which are provable by evidence of reputation.*

Cross Reference to Federal Rule 803(23)

Explanation

NOTE: This section must be read in conjunction with Rule 803(19) and 803(20). Rule 803(23) only permits admissibility of such evidence where the judgment proves facts which would be provable by reputation evidence.

Hearsay Exception:
Judgment of Previous Conviction

Objections

- *I object. The question calls for a hearsay answer.*

- *I move to strike the answer as hearsay.*

Responses

- *This statement is admissible as a judgment of previous conviction pursuant to Rule 803(22). I have shown through a certified record, or the testimony of* (insert name of witness) *that this statement is evidence of:*

  - *a final judgment,*

  - *entered after a trial or upon a plea of guilty,*

  - *adjudging a person guilty of a crime punishable by either death or imprisonment for more than one year,*

  - *which is offered to prove a fact essential to sustain the judgment,*

  - *(in a criminal prosecution) which is the conviction of someone other than the accused.*

Cross Reference to Federal Rule 803(22)

Explanation

The judgment of a prior conviction for a crime which carries a sentence of death or at least one year in prison is admissible as against a hearsay exception in civil cases where it is offered against the person convicted, in a later case for the proof of a fact essential to sustain the judgment of conviction. Such conviction is admissible for its truth in a second case only against the person convicted. In a criminal case, this exception only allows admissibility of the judgment as proof of the conviction concerning non-defendant witnesses, unless it is offered only for impeachment purposes.

G

H

Hearsay Exception:
Learned Treatises

Objections

- *I object. The question calls for a hearsay answer.*

- *I move to strike the answer as hearsay.*

Responses

- *This statement is admissible as a statement contained in a learned treatise pursuant to Rule 803(18). I have shown through the testimony of* (insert name of witness) *that:*

   (on direct examination)

   - *the expert witness has relied on the statement,* or

   (on cross examination)

   - *I have called the statement to the attention of the expert,* and
   - *the statement is contained in a published treatise, periodical, or pamphlet on a subject of history, medicine, or other science or art,*
   - *which has been established as a reliable authority by the testimony or admission of the expert witness, by other expert testimony, or by judicial notice.*

Cross Reference to Federal Rule 803(18)

Explanation

A learned treatise is a book or article established as a reliable authority on a matter, ordinarily the subject of expert opinion, which is called to the attention of an expert witness on cross examination, or which is relied upon by the expert in direct examination. A foundation for the learned treatise may be laid through the expert who is on the stand, through some other expert, or through the taking of judicial notice by the trial judge of the learned nature of the writing. The learned treatise is admissible to either support or attack the testimony of an expert witness. Note that the treatise may only be read to the jury and may not be received as an exhibit. If admitted, the statement contained in the learned treatise may be read into evidence, but may not be admitted as an exhibit.

G

H

Hearsay Exception:
Market Reports and
Commercial Publications

Objection

- *I object. The document is an out-of-court state-ment and is therefore hearsay.*

Response

- *This statement is admissible as a market report or commercial publication pursuant to Rule 803(17). I have shown the document is:*

  - *a market quotation, tabulation, list, direc-tory, or other published compilation,*

  - *which is generally used and relied upon by the public or persons in particular occupations.*

Cross Reference to Federal Rule 803(17)

Explanation

Market reports or commercial publications are out-of-court statements which compile facts or data used by either the general public or by per-sons in particular professions or occupations and which are relied upon for the purposes of carrying out their daily businesses.

Hearsay Exception: Marriage, Baptismal, and Similar Certificates

Objection

- *I object. The document is an out-of-court statement offered for its truth and is hearsay.*

Response

- *This statement is admissible as a marriage, baptismal, or similar certificate pursuant to Rule 803(12). I have shown through the testimony of* (insert name of witness) *that this is a statement of fact:*

  - *contained in a certificate which shows the maker performed a marriage or other similar ceremony,*

  - *made by a clergyman, public official, or other person authorized by law or the practices of a religious organization to perform the act certified,* and

  - *which purports to be issued at the time of the act or within a reasonable time thereafter.*

Cross Reference to Federal Rule 803(12)

Explanation

Examples of facts which could be proved by the use of Rule 803(12) are paternity through a baptismal certificate and marriage through a marriage certificate.

G

H

Hearsay Exception:
Present Sense Impression

Objections

- *I object. The question calls for a hearsay answer.*

- *I move to strike the answer as hearsay.*

Response

- *This statement is admissible as a present sense impression pursuant to Rule 803(1). I have shown through the testimony of* (insert name of witness) *that the statement describes or explains an event or condition, and was made:*

  - *while the declarant was perceiving the event or condition,* or

  - *immediately thereafter.*

Cross Reference to Federal Rule 803(1)

Explanation

A present sense impression is an out-of-court statement which describes or explains an occurrence or condition made at the time the declarant was perceiving the occurrence or condition, or immediately thereafter. The event described in the statement need not be exciting or startling. The guarantee of reliability for this hearsay exception is spontaneity or contemporaneity.

Hearsay Exception: Public Records and Reports

Objections

- *I object. The question calls for a hearsay answer.*

- *I move to strike the answer as hearsay.*

- *(In a criminal case) I object. The report is not admissible against a criminal defendant.*

Responses

- *The out-of-court statement is admissible under the hearsay exception (Rule 803(8)) for public records and reports. I have shown through the testimony of* (insert name of witness) *that:*

  - *the document is a record, report, statement, or data compilation,*

  - *of a public office or agency setting forth*

    - *the activities of the office or agency,* or

    - *the matters observed pursuant to duty imposed by law as to which matters there was a duty to report.*

Cross Reference to Federal Rule 803(8)

Explanation

Such public records and reports are admissible unless the source of information or other circumstances indicate a lack of trustworthiness in the making or keeping of such records or reports. These records or reports gain their reliability from the public duty or the duty imposed by law which accompanies the maker's obligation to observe and record events. Conclusions reached by the agency preparing the report are admissible where accompanied by the factual findings on which the conclusions are based. Records otherwise qualifying for admission pursuant to this exception are not admissible in a criminal case against the defendant when they are matters reported by law enforcement authorities.

G
H

Hearsay Exception:
Records of Documents Affecting an Interest in Property

Objection

- *I object. The document is an out-of-court statement offered for its truth and is therefore hearsay.*

Response

- *The statement is admissible as a record of a document affecting an interest in property pursuant to Rule 803(14). I have shown through the testimony of* (insert name of witness) *that:*
  - *this is a record of a public office,* and
  - *an applicable statute authorizes the recording of documents of that kind in such office.*

Cross Reference to Federal Rule 803(14)

Explanation

A record of a document affecting an interest in property is an out-of-court writing which either relates to or establishes interest in property. It must be shown to be kept in an office which has the statutory authority to keep such records.

Hearsay Exception:
Recorded Recollection

Objections

- *I object. The question calls for a hearsay answer.*

- *I move to strike the answer as hearsay.*

Response

- *This statement is admissible as recorded recollection pursuant to Rule 803(5). I have shown through the testimony of* (insert name of witness) *that it is:*

  - *a memorandum or record concerning a matter,*

  - *about which a witness once had knowledge,*

  - *but now has insufficient recollection to enable the witness to testify fully and accurately,* and

  - *shown to have been made or adopted by the witness when the matter was fresh in the witness's memory and to reflect that knowledge correctly.*

Cross Reference to Federal Rule 803(5)

Explanation

Past recollection recorded must be distinguished from present recollection refreshed. Though both require a failure of memory as a predicate, present recollection refreshed presents no hearsay problem at all. Present recollection refreshed refers to a situation where a witness has a failure of memory. The witness is then shown the item which serves to refresh his or her recollection; the item is then removed from the witness, and the witness testifies from a refreshed recollection. Past recollection recorded refers to a document created by the witness, or at the witness's direction, when the matter was fresh in the witness's mind so as to accurately reflect that knowledge. Note that the document may only be read to the jury, and may not be received as an exhibit.

Hearsay Exception: Records of Regularly Conducted Activity (Business Records)

Objections

- *I object. The question calls for a hearsay answer.*

- *I move to strike the answer as hearsay.*

Responses

- *This statement is admissible as a business record pursuant to Rule 803(6). I have shown through the testimony of* (insert name of witness) *who is a custodian of the record or person who has knowledge of the record-keeping system or by certificaiton under Rule 902(11) or (12), that the statement is contained in a:*

(For manually entered records)

- *memorandum, report, record, or data compilation,*

- *recording acts, events, conditions, opinions, or diagnoses,*

- *made at or near the time the acts or events took place,*

- *by or from information transmitted by one with personal knowledge of the event or act,*
- *where such record is kept in the course of a regularly conducted business activity,* and
- *it was the regular practice of the business to make such record.*

(For computer-generated records, repeat the above steps and add)

- *the computer and the program used are generally accepted in the field,*
- *the computer was in good working order at relevant times,* and
- *the computer operator possessed the knowledge and training to correctly operate the computer.*

Cross Reference to Federal Rule 803(6)

Explanation

A record of regularly conducted activity, known in the common law as a business record, is a writing or compilation of data which records activities or happenings, including opinions, made in the course of a regularly conducted activity, and kept in the course of such activity, and created by and from a person with personal knowledge of the contents of the record, at or near the time of the event recorded. The exception covers records of regularly conducted activities on the part of all entities, whether or not they are formed for the purpose of making a profit. The foundation for the Rule 803(6) record may be laid either through the testimony of a live witness or through the certification process described in Rules 902(11) and (12).

G

H

Hearsay Exception:
Records of Religious Organizations

Objection

- *I object. The record is an out-of-court statement offered for its truth and is hearsay.*

Response

- *This statement is admissible as a record of a religious organization pursuant to Rule 803 (11). I have shown through the testimony of* (insert name of witness) *that the statement:*
  - *is one of personal or family history,* and
  - *is contained in a regularly kept record of a religious organization.*

Cross Reference to Federal Rule 803(11)

Explanation

This rule creates a hearsay exception for records of personal and family history so long as such records are maintained in a regularly kept record of some religious organization.

Hearsay Exception:
Records of Vital Statistics

Objection

- *I object. The record is an out-of-court statement offered for its truth and is hearsay.*

Response

- *The out-of-court statement is admissible pursuant to Rule 803(9) for records of a vital statistic in that it:*
  - *is a record regarding a vital statistic*
  - *which records a report made to a public official required by law to keep such a record.*

Cross Reference to Federal Rule 803(9)

Explanation

As with other out-of-court writings which are offered pursuant to a hearsay exception, records of vital statistics must be authenticated either through the testimony of the public officer who creates and maintains the records or, more easily, by the proffer of a certified copy of the public record pursuant to Rule 902(4).

Hearsay Exception:
Reputation as to Character

Objections

- *I object. The question calls for a hearsay answer.*

- *I move to strike the answer as hearsay.*

Response

- *This statement is admissible as reputation as to character pursuant to Rule 803(21). I have shown through the testimony of* (insert name of witness) *that this is a statement of:*
  - *reputation of a person's character*
  - *among associates or in the community.*

Cross Reference to Federal Rule 803(21)

Explanation

Reputation is a collection of hearsay. Reputation of a person's character which is found among his or her associates in some community is admissible as a hearsay exception, subject to the relevance requirements of Rules 404, 405, and 608.

Hearsay Exception: Reputation Concerning Boundaries or General History

Objections

- *I object. The question calls for a hearsay answer.*

- *I move to strike the answer as hearsay.*

Response

- *This statement is admissible as a statement of reputation concerning boundaries or general history pursuant to Rule 803(20). I have shown through the testimony of* (insert name of witness) *that this is a statement of reputation:*

  - *in a community,*

  - *arising before the controversy,*

  - *as to boundaries of, or customs affecting, lands in the community,* or

  - *as to events of general history important to the community or state or nation in which located.*

Cross Reference to Federal Rule 803(20)

Explanation

Reputation concerning boundaries or general history involves a collection of hearsay drawn from a community regarding events of general import or knowledge in that community. The exception gains reliability from the force of general community knowledge.

G

H

Hearsay Exception: Reputation Concerning Personal or Family History

Objections

- *I object. The question calls for a hearsay answer.*

- *I move to strike the answer as hearsay.*

G

H

Response

- *This statement is admissible as a statement of reputation concerning personal or family history pursuant to Rule 803(19). I have shown through the testimony of* (insert name of witness) *that this is a statement of reputation:*

  - *among members of one's family,* or

  - *among one's associates,* or

  - *in the community,*

  - *concerning a person's adoption, birth, marriage, divorce, death, legitimacy, relationship by blood, adoption or marriage, ancestry, or other similar fact of personal or family history.*

Cross Reference to Federal Rule 803(19)

Explanation

The witness who testifies concerning the reputation clearly must be familiar with that reputation which is shown by (a) the witness being a member of the relevant family, community, or group of associates, and by (b) the witness's familiarity with the reputation, having either heard it discussed or taken part in such discussions.

G

H

Hearsay Exception:
Requirement of Unavailability
for Rule 804 Hearsay Exceptions

Objections

- *I object. The question calls for a hearsay answer.*

- *I move to strike the answer as hearsay.*

Responses

- *The out-of-court statement meets* (insert the appropriate 804(b) exception). *The declarant is unavailable because the declarant:*

  - *is exempted from testifying concerning the subject of the statement by ruling by the court on the ground of privilege, or*

  - *persists in refusing to testify concerning the subject of the statement despite a court order to do so, or*

  - *testifies to a lack of memory on the subject of the statement, or*

  - *is unable to testify at the hearing because of death or illness, or*

  - *is absent from the hearing and I, as the proponent of the declarant's statement, have been unable to procure the declarant's attendance through process or other means, or*

- (Provide any other reason for the witness's absence.)

Cross Reference to Federal Rule 804(a), (b)

Explanation

NOTE: Unavailability of a hearsay declarant does not, in and of itself, create an exception to the hearsay rule. Unavailability is merely the first requirement for all Rule 804 exceptions to the hearsay rule. The types of unavailability listed in Rule 804(a) are not the exclusive circumstances of unavailability. Rather, this rule lists circumstances which *per se* amount to unavailability, but fails to exclude any other legitimate showing of unavailability which the trial judge determines acceptable pursuant to Rule 804.

Hearsay Exception:
Residual Exception

Objections

- *I object. The question calls for a hearsay answer.*

- *I move to strike the answer as hearsay.*

Response

- *The statement is admissible pursuant to the residual exception to the hearsay rule contained in Rule 807. I have shown through the testimony of* (insert name of witness) *that:*

  - *the statement is not specifically covered by any of the enumerated hearsay exceptions,* and

  - *the statement has circumstantial guarantees of trustworthiness equivalent to that of the enumerated exceptions,* and

  - *the statement is offered as evidence of a material fact,* and

  - *the statement is more probative on the point for which it is offered than any other evidence which I can procure through reasonable efforts,* and

- *the general purposes of these rules in the interests of justice will be best served by the admission of this statement into evidence,* and

- *I have given the adverse parties notice sufficiently in advance of trial or hearing of my intention to offer the statements so as to afford them a fair opportunity to prepare to meet it.*

Cross Reference to Federal Rule 807

Explanation

The residual exceptions to the hearsay rule provide identical catch-all provisions which permit the admission of hearsay where, although not fitting any of the enumerated exceptions, the proffered hearsay possesses guarantees of trustworthiness equivalent to that of the enumerated exceptions and is more probative of the fact for which it is offered than any other available, admissible evidence.

Hearsay Exception: Statement Against Interest

Objections

- *I object. The question calls for a hearsay answer.*

- *I move to strike the answer as hearsay.*

Responses

- *This statement is admissible as a statement against interest pursuant to Rule 804(b)(3). I have shown through the testimony of* (insert name of witness) *that the statement:*

  - *was made by a declarant who is now unavailable pursuant to Rule 804(a),* and

    - *was at the time of its making, so far contrary to the declarant's pecuniary or proprietary interest,* or

    - *so far tended to subject the declarant to criminal or civil liability,* or

    - *to render invalid a claim by the declarant against another,* and

  - *that a reasonable person in the declarant's position would not have made this statement unless he or she believed it to be true,* and

- (If the statement tends to expose the declarant to criminal liability and is offered to exculpate the accused) *corroborating circumstances clearly indicate the trustworthiness of the statement.*

Cross Reference to Federal Rule 804(b)(3)

Explanation

NOTE: There is a special treatment for a statement against criminal or penal interest, where offered to exculpate and excuse, which requires that there be corroborating circumstances which indicate the truthfulness or reliability of the statement against criminal liability or criminal interest.

Hearsay Exception: Statements in Ancient Documents

Objection

- *I object. The statement is contained in an out-of-court writing offered for its truth, which is hearsay.*

Response

G
H

- *This statement is admissible as a statement contained in an ancient document pursuant to Rule 803(16). I have shown through the testimony of* (insert name of witness) *that the statement is contained in:*
  - *a document in existence twenty years or more,*
  - *the authenticity of which is established.*

Cross Reference to Federal Rule 803(16)

Explanation

The foundational requirements for establishing authenticity of an ancient document require the condition of the document to create no suspicion regarding its authenticity, the document must have been kept in a place where it likely would be kept if it were authentic, and it must indeed have been in existence for at least twenty years at the time of its proffer at trial.

Hearsay Exception:
Statements in Documents
Affecting an Interest in Property

Objections

- *I object. The question calls for a hearsay answer.*

- *I move to strike the answer as hearsay.*

Response

- *This statement is admissible pursuant to Rule 803(15) as a statement in a document affecting an interest in property. I have shown through the testimony of* (insert name of witness) *that:*

  - *the statement is contained in a document purporting to establish or affect an interest in property,*

  - *the matter stated was relevant to the purpose of the document,* and

  - *dealings with the property since the document was made have not been inconsistent with the truth of the statement or the purpose of the document.*

Cross Reference to Federal Rule 803(15)

Explanation

The requirements for qualification of admissibility under this rule are as follows. First, the factual statement contained in the document must relate to or be relevant to the purpose of the document; second, the document would only be admissible so long as the dealings with the property have not been inconsistent with the truth of the statement or the purport of the document which was offered.

G
H

Hearsay Exception: Statement of Personal or Family History

Objections

- *I object. The question calls for a hearsay answer.*

- *I move to strike the answer as hearsay.*

Responses

- *This statement is admissible as a statement of personal or family history pursuant to Rule 804(b)(4). I have shown through the testimony of* (insert name of witness) *that:*

  - *the declarant is now unavailable pursuant to Rule 804(a),* and

  - *the statement concerns the declarant's own birth, adoption, marriage, divorce, legitimacy, relationship by blood, adoption, or marriage, ancestry or other similar fact of personal or family history,*

  - *even though the declarant had no means of acquiring personal knowledge of the matter stated,* or

  - *the statement concerns the foregoing matters, as well as the death of another person, where the declarant was related to the other person by blood, adoption, or marriage, or was so intimately associated with the other's family as to be likely to give accurate information concerning the matter declared.*

Cross Reference to Federal Rule 804(b)(4)

Explanation

NOTE: The requirement of declarant's personal knowledge which ordinarily must be apparent from the circumstances of the making of a declarant's admissible hearsay statement is explicitly dispensed with pursuant to Rule 804(b)(4).

Hearsay Exception: Statements for Purposes of Medical Diagnosis or Treatment

Objections

- *I object. The question calls for a hearsay answer.*

- *I move to strike the answer as hearsay.*

Responses

- *This statement is admissible as a statement for purposes of medical diagnosis or treatment pursuant to Rule 803(4). I have shown through the testimony of* (insert name of witness) *that the statement:*

  - *was made for purposes of medical diagnosis or treatment,* and

  - *was made for describing medical history; or to describe past or present symptoms, pain, or sensations; or to describe the inception or general character of the cause or external source thereof,* and

  - *was reasonably pertinent to diagnosis or treatment.*

Cross Reference to Federal Rule 803(4)

Explanation

Statements made to persons other than those immediately able to render medical assistance can qualify for this hearsay exception if made for purposes of obtaining medical diagnosis or treatment. However, statements of causation or the external source of the physical condition mentioned in the out-of-court statement will only be admissible if pertinent to the medical diagnosis or treatment. The key inquiry is whether the statement is pathologically germane to the diagnosis or treatment of a medical patient. Where and how an injury occurs is usually germane; who caused the injury usually is not.

G
H

Hearsay Exception: Statement Under Belief of Impending Death

Objections

- *I object. The question calls for a hearsay answer.*

- *I move to strike the answer as hearsay.*

Response

- *The statement is admissible as one made under belief of impending death pursuant to Rule 804(b)(2). I have shown through the testimony of* (insert name of witness) *that the statement:*

  - *was made by a declarant who is now unavailable pursuant to Rule 804(a),*

  - *is offered in a prosecution for homicide or civil action or proceeding,*

  - *was made by the declarant while believing that death was imminent,* and

  - *concerns the causes or circumstances of what the declarant believed to be impending death.*

Cross Reference to Federal Rule 804(b)(2)

Explanation

Unlike the common law, the Federal Rule does not require a declarant to die as a foundational requirement to the offering of a statement under belief of impending death. The guarantee of reliability is found in the reasonable belief on the part of the declarant that he or she is about to die.

G

H

Hearsay Exception:
Then Existing Mental or
Emotional Condition

Objections

- *I object. The question calls for a hearsay answer.*

- *I move to strike the answer as hearsay.*

Responses

- *This statement is admissible as a statement of a then existing mental or emotional condition pursuant to Rule 803(3). I have shown through the testimony of* (insert name of witness) *that the statement:*
  - *is of the declarant's then existing:*
    - *state of mind,* or
    - *emotions,* or
    - *sensation,* and
  - *it does not include a statement of memory or belief offered to prove the fact remembered or believed,* or
  - *it relates to the execution, revocation, identification, or terms of declarant's will.*

Cross Reference to Federal Rule 803(3)

Explanation

It is critical to note that only statements regarding a present mental or emotional condition fit within the exception. A statement regarding a past mental or emotional condition will not be admissible because there is no substantial guarantee of reliability, except when the statement relates to the declarant's will.

G

H

Hearsay Exception:
Then Existing Physical Condition

Objections

- *I object. The statement is hearsay.*
- *I move to strike the answer as hearsay.*

Response

- *This statement is admissible as a statement of a then existing physical condition pursuant to Rule 803(3). I have shown through the testimony of* (insert name of witness) *that the statement:*
  - *is of the declarant's then existing physical condition,* and
  - *does not include a statement of memory or belief to prove the fact remembered or believed.*

Cross Reference to Federal Rule 803(3)

Explanation

A statement of a then existing physical condition gains its reliability from the contemporaneity of the statement and the existence of the physical condition described by the declarant. It is critical to note that only statements regarding present physical condition come within the exception. A statement regarding a past condition will not be admissible because there is no substantial guarantee of reliability.

Impeachment:
Bias, Prejudice, Interest, and Improper Motive

Objections

- (To questions posed on cross examination) *I object. Counsel is attempting to impeach the witness on improper grounds. The testimony attempted to be elicited is irrelevant.*

- (To extrinsic evidence) *I object. Counsel has not laid the proper foundation for use of extrinsic evidence to impeach. The witness whom counsel is attempting to impeach:*
  - *has not yet been called as a witness,* or
  - *was not confronted with the alleged bias, interest, or improper motive on cross examination,* or
  - *was confronted with the alleged bias, prejudice, interest, or improper motive, but did not deny its existence.*

Responses

- (To an objection posed on cross examination) *I am attempting to show that the witness:*
  - *is biased,* or
  - *is prejudiced,* or

- *has an interest in the outcome of the case,* or

- *has an improper motive for giving testimony.*

- (To an objection posed to extrinsic evidence)

  - (Where the witness with the alleged bias, prejudice, interest, or improper motive has not already testified) *The witness has been listed as a witness by my opponent and I offer this evidence conditionally to avoid recalling the witness presently on the stand at a later time.*

  - (Where the witness with the alleged bias, prejudice, interest, or improper motive has already testified) *I confronted* (insert name of witness) *with his or her* (bias, prejudice, interest, or improper motive) *during cross examination when I asked* (insert question), *and he or she denied it.*

Cross Reference to Federal Rule

[There is no federal rule that specifically deals with bias, prejudice, interest, or improper motive. These are traditional areas of impeachment that fall within the general impeachment provision of Rule 607.]

Explanation

Bias, prejudice, interest, and improper motive are particularly fertile areas for impeachment and are probably the most typical areas of impeachment with most witnesses. They all depend on the relationship of the witness with one of the parties or the subject of the litigation.

I
J
K

Impeachment:
Character Evidence

Objections

- *I object. The character witness has insufficient knowledge of the witness's character to give an opinion.*

- *I object. The character witness has insufficient knowledge of the witness's reputation for dishonesty to report that opinion to the court.*

Responses

- *A sufficient foundation has been laid to demonstrate the character witness's sufficient familiarity with:*
  - *the witness's character for dishonesty,* or
  - *the witness's reputation for honesty in the community.*

Cross Reference to Federal Rule 608(a), (b)

Explanation

A witness may be impeached by opinion or reputation testimony that the witness has bad character for honesty. Once a witness has been impeached by evidence of dishonest character, such witness may be rehabilitated by the calling of a character witness who will testify as to the witness's character for honesty or truthfulness by way of opinion or reputation evidence.

Impeachment:
Memory

Objection

- *I object. The question seeks to elicit irrelevant information; the question involves improper impeachment.*

Response

- *The question calls for an answer that will show the witness's inability to remember the events about which testimony has been given. This is proper cross examination.*

Cross Reference to Federal Rule

[There is no federal rule that specifically deals with impeachment with regard to faulty memory. See Rule 607.]

Explanation

A witness may be impeached by showing that the witness has an impaired ability to remember the events in question or by showing the unlikelihood that the witness can actually remember those items about which testimony is given. This form of impeachment is often coupled with impeachment showing bias, prejudice, etc.

Impeachment: Perception

Objection

- *I object. The question seeks to elicit irrelevant information. The question involves improper impeachment.*

Response

- *The question calls for an answer that will show the witness's inability to perceive. This is proper cross examination.*

Cross Reference to Federal Rule

[There is no federal rule that specifically deals with impeachment regarding the ability to perceive. See Rule 607.]

Explanation

A witness may be impeached by showing an impaired ability to perceive the events in question. Such impeachment is typically accomplished by showing the time, place, and circumstances in which the perception occurs, from which the lawyer can argue and the jury can infer that the witness is not worthy of belief. Matters of perception include the ability to see, hear, smell, or feel some particular matter or item in question.

Impeachment:
Prior Convictions
(Civil Cases)

Objections

- *I object. The proffered conviction is neither for a crime which carries at least one year in prison nor is it a conviction for a crime involving dishonesty or false statement.*

- *I object. The date of conviction and the witness's release date from sentence for the conviction occurred more than ten years ago **and** written notice has not been given **and/or** the probative value of the conviction on the issue of credibility does not substantially outweigh the prejudice to a party of admitting such conviction.*

- *I object.* (For Rule 609(a)(1) crimes) *The prejudicial effect of the conviction substantially outweighs the probative value of the evidence on the issue of credibility **and/or** the admission of the evidence will lead to confusion of the issues or will mislead the jury.*

Responses

- *The proffered conviction is a felony conviction **or** a crime involving dishonesty or false statement.*

- *Though the proffered conviction and the witness's release date occurred longer than ten years ago, written notice has been given **and** the probative value of the conviction on the issue of credibility substantially outweighs the prejudice to the opposing party.*

- *The prejudice to the opposing party does not substantially outweigh the probative value of the conviction on the issue of the witness's credibility. The jury will not be misled or confused as to the import of the evidence of conviction as it is limited solely to the issue of the witness's credibility.*

Cross Reference to Federal Rule 609(a), (b), (c), (d), (e)

Explanation

Rule 609(a)(1) which deals with the admissibility of convictions for impeachment purposes for crimes not covered by Rule 609(a)(2), but which carry a potential sentence of death or imprisonment in excess of one year, was amended in 1990. Rule 609(a)(1) now provides, unequivocally, that the admission of evidence of such convictions shall be determined in civil cases by Rule 403 consideration of the balance between prejudicial effect and probative value. The trial judge now has discretion to exclude other admissible 609(a)(1) convictions, if the prejudicial effect of the conviction substantially outweighs the probative value of the conviction as it bears on the issue of the credibility of witnesses.

Rule 609(a)(2) is unequivocal in mandating the admission of prior conviction evidence for impeachment purposes where the conviction is for a crime of dishonesty or false statement. Dishonesty crimes, also known as crimes in the nature of crimen falsi, will typically include any theft crime and exclude any crime of violence. There is no discretion in the trial judge to exclude evidence of 609(a)(2) convictions.

I
J
K

Impeachment:
Prior Convictions
(Criminal Cases)

Objections

- (Where offered against any witness other than the criminal defendant) *I object. The conviction offered to impeach is neither for a crime which carries a penalty of at least one year in prison or death, nor for a crime of dishonesty or false statement. Even if the conviction offered to impeach is for a felony, the prejudicial effect to a party substantially outweighs the probative value of the conviction on the issue of the credibility of the witness.*

- *I object because the date of the proffered conviction and the witness's release date from his sentence occurred more than ten years ago, written notice has not been given, and / or the probative value of the conviction on the issue of credibility does not substantially outweigh the prejudice to a party of admitting such conviction.*

- (Where offered against the criminal defendant-witness) *I object to the introduction of this conviction because the probative value of the conviction on the issue of credibility does not outweigh the prejudice to the defendant.*

Responses

- (Where offered against any witness other than the criminal defendant) *The proffered conviction is for a Rule 609(a)(1) crime, and its prejudicial effect to any party in the case does not substantially outweigh its probative value on the issue of the credibility of the witness.*

- (Where offered against the criminal defendant) *The proffered conviction is for a Rule 609(a)(1) crime and its probative value does outweigh the prejudicial effect to the defendant.*

- *The proffered conviction is for activity involving dishonesty or false statement.*

- *Though the proffered conviction and the witness's release date occurred longer than ten years ago, written notice has been given and the probative value of the conviction on the issue of the witness's credibility substantially outweighs any purported prejudice.*

Cross Reference to Federal Rule 609(a), (b), (c), (d), (e)

Explanation

As with the use of convictions for impeachment in civil cases, Rule 609 in criminal cases dispenses with any balancing of probative value against prejudice in the offer of a conviction for a crime of dishonesty or false statement. Thus, such convictions must be admitted against any witness including a criminal defendant. Where, however, a criminal defendant would be impeached with a conviction for a crime that carries a penalty of at least one year in prison that does not involve dishonesty or false statement, Rule 609(a) requires the court to perform a balance which is different from Rule 403 balance and tilts away from admissibility. Such conviction will only be admitted against a criminal defendant where the court finds that the probative value of the conviction on the defendant's credibility outweighs the prejudice to the defendant. The obvious prejudice to a criminal defendant lies in the jury's inclination to find a defendant guilty of the crime charged because of his prior record. Arguably, the similarity between the charged offense and the prior conviction magnifies the prejudicial impact of the prior conviction because of the jury's almost inevitable sense that one who once committed a particular sort of offense is likely to commit a similar offense again. Whatever the common sense likelihood of such a notion, it is an impermissible inference for a fact-finder to make.

The term *crime of dishonesty or false statement* includes crimes where it can readily be determined that the establishment of the elements fo the crime required proof or admission of an act of dishonesty or false statement by the witness who is being impeached. According to the Advisory Note, "[o]rdinarily, the statement. Wher the deceitful nature of the crim is not apparent from the statute and the face of judgment,...a proponent may offer such as an indictment, a statement of admitted facts, or jury instructions in order to demonstrate that proof of an act of dishonesty or false statement was required for conviction.

A witness in a criminal case, other than the criminal defendant, is treated like a witness in a civil case for purposes of Rule 609(a) and impeachment of witnesses may be excluded on Rule 403 grounds.

I
J
K

Impeachment:
Prior Inconsistent Statements

Objections

- *I object. The proffered statement is not inconsistent with the witness's testimony and is irrelevant.*

- (For impeachment by extrinsic evidence of a prior inconsistent statement) *I object. A proper foundation has not been laid for introduction of extrinsic evidence of a prior inconsistent statement in that the witness my adversary is attempting to impeach has not been given an opportunity to explain or deny the alleged inconsistent statement.*

Responses

(For impeachment by prior inconsistent statement on cross examination)

- *The witness has testified during direct examination that* (insert testimony) *and this statement is inconsistent with the thrust of the direct testimony.*

- *The witness testified during direct examination that* (insert testimony) *and this statement is inconsistent in that it omits facts testified to on direct examination.*

(For impeachment by extrinsic evidence of a prior inconsistent statement)

- *The witness denied making a prior inconsistent statement during cross examination.*

- *This prior inconsistent statement is an admission of a party opponent pursuant to Rule 801 (d)(2) and therefore the witness need not be given an opportunity to explain or deny the prior inconsistent statement.*

Cross Reference to Federal Rule 613(a), (b)

Explanation

The federal rules do not require a formal foundation for impeachment by a prior inconsistent statement. Good tactics dictate, however, that counsel show, by way of foundation, the time, place, and circumstances of the inconsistent statement for maximum effect. In addition, it is tactically advisable to give a copy of written inconsistent statements to the witness who is about to be impeached. This is especially important when the prior statement is inconsistent by omission.

Impeachment:
Specific Instances of Misconduct

Objections

- (On cross examination) *I object. The specific instance of conduct does not show lack of honesty or truth-telling ability.*

- (To extrinsic evidence, written or oral) *I object. Extrinsic evidence of specific instances of conduct relating to honesty is inadmissible.*

Response

- *The specific instance of conduct shows lack of truth-telling ability in that* (insert reason or testimony).

Cross Reference to Federal Rule 608(b)

Explanation

Specific instances of conduct that show, without reference to the subject matter of the lawsuit, that a witness is not a truth-teller are admissible pursuant to Rule 608(b). Extrinsic evidence of instances of misconduct relating to honesty is not admissible.

Insurance Against Liability

Objection

- *I object that the proponent is offering evidence of liability insurance on the issue of negligence or other wrongful conduct. I move for a mistrial.*

Response

- *This evidence of liability insurance is not offered on the issue of negligence, but to show:*
  - *ownership,*
  - *agency,*
  - *control,*
  - *bias,* or
  - *some other purpose other than liability.*

Cross Reference to Federal Rule 411

Explanation

Contrary to common belief, the mere mention of the defendant's being insured against liability is not necessarily inadmissible, nor need it lead to a mistrial. Evidence of insurance generally is not admissible only on the issues of liability and the ability of a party to pay damages.

Judicial Notice

Objection

- *I object to the court judicially noticing* (insert fact offered) *in that*
  - *it is not generally known in this jurisdiction,* and/or
  - *it is open to dispute and not capable of ready and certain verification.*

Responses

I J K

- *Judicial notice of* (insert fact offered) *is appropriate because:*
  - *the fact is generally known by people in this local jurisdiction and to require other proof would waste the time of the court,* or
  - *it is capable of ready and certain verification by resort to authoritative sources which have been provided to the court.*

Cross Reference to Federal Rule 201

Explanation

Where the court is provided with authoritative sources which prove the fact, judicial notice, on request, is mandatory. The court may judicially notice an appropriate fact on its own motion. The opposing party has the right to be heard concerning the propriety of judicial notice.

Lay Opinion Evidence

Objections

- *I object. The question calls for an opinion.*

- *I move to strike the answer because it is stated in the form of opinion.*

Response

- *This is permissible opinion from a lay witness because it is rationally based on the perception of the witness and would help the trier of fact to understand the witness's testimony and determine a fact in issue in this lawsuit.*

Cross Reference to Federal Rules 701, 704

Explanation

Lay opinion is generally allowed where its admission makes the jury's fact-finding easier and more accurate. A typical admissible lay opinion occurs where a witness provides an inference to the jury which takes the place of describing a series of perceptions which in common experience add up to a rather ordinary inference or characterization (e.g., testimony that someone looked happy, sad, confused, angry, etc.).

Leading Questions

Objection

- *I object to the question as leading.*

Responses

- *The question does not suggest the answer to the witness.*

- *Leading questions are permitted:*
  - *on preliminary matters, or*
  - *when necessary to develop the witness's testimony, or*
  - *because the witness is hostile, is an adverse party, or is identified with an adverse party.*

Cross Reference to Federal Rule 611(c)

L
M
N

Explanation

A leading question is one which suggests the desired answer to the witness so that it puts the desired answer in the witness's mouth or is one which makes it unclear as to whether the witness or the lawyer is testifying.

Misquoting the Witness

Objection

- *I object. Counsel is misquoting the witness. The witness has testified to* (insert substance of witness's testimony).

Response

- *The witness previously testified to* (insert substance of witness's testimony).

Cross Reference to Federal Rule

[There is no federal rule that specifically covers forms of questions. The court has discretion to sustain the objection pursuant to Rule 611(a).]

Explanation

This objection is designed to prevent opposing counsel from shading the testimony of the witness as it had previously been rendered. The objection can serve as a reminder to the witness to listen carefully to opposing counsel's questions before answering.

Narratives

Objections

- *I object. The question calls for a narrative response.*

- *I object. The witness is testifying in the form of a narrative.*

Response

- *The witness is testifying to relevant and admissible matters.*

Cross Reference to Federal Rule

[There is no federal rule that specifically covers forms of questions. The court has discretion to sustain the objection pursuant to Rule 611(a).]

Explanation

This objection seeks to prevent the situation where counsel is not provided with notice by the question as to potential objectionable testimony by a witness. The best tactic for objecting counsel is to state, at the bench, the reasons for the objection; that is, to prevent inadmissible evidence from being heard by the jury and possibly cemented by a motion to strike. At the first instance when the witness testifies to inadmissible evidence during the narrative, opposing counsel should move to strike, approach the bench, and ask the judge to reconsider the objection to testimony in a narrative form.

Non-Responsive Answers

Objection

- *I move to strike the answer of the witness as non-responsive.*

Responses

- (If the objection is made by questioning counsel) *The answer of the witness is responsive to the question. The question put to the witness was* (insert the form of the question).

- (If the objection is made by opposing counsel) *I accept the answer.*

Cross Reference to Federal Rule

[There is no federal rule that specifically covers forms of questions. The court has discretion to sustain the objection pursuant to Rule 611(a).]

Explanation

The objection of non-responsiveness belongs only to questioning counsel. Answers which exceed the scope of the question may be the subject of a motion to strike by opposing counsel on specific substantive grounds. Opposing counsel may also object to the testimony of a witness as testimony in a narrative form which is treated under "narratives" in this text.

Objections

Objection

(See specific objections under appropriate captions in this text for forms of objections.)

Responses

(See specific responses under appropriate captions in this text for forms of responses.)

Cross Reference to Federal Rule 103

Explanation

Generally, failure to object waives appellate consideration of any error in the admission of evidence at trial. Objections must state the specific ground for exclusion of evidence unless the ground for objection is obvious. Objections must be timely in that they must be stated as soon as the objectionable nature of the question or answer becomes apparent.

Where the court makes a definitive ruling, *in limine*, to admit or exclude evidence, there is no need to renew the objection or offer of proof at trial when the evidence is or would have been offered. However, where the court rules, *in limine*, to admit evidence of a prior conviction to impeach a criminal defendant, failure of the defendant to testify waives the objection to the admission of the impeaching conviction.

O
P
9

Offers of Proof

Forms of the Offer

- Ask the witness to state for the record, outside the hearing of the jury, what the witness's testimony would have been if the judge had not excluded it; or

- A statement by the counsel who attempted to offer the witness's statement, which provides the substance of what the witness's testimony would have been, but for the adverse ruling; or

- A prepared written statement of the witness's testimony which would have been given, but for the adverse ruling.

Cross Reference to Federal Rules 103(a)(2), 103(b)

Explanation

OPG

The offer of proof can be made in one of three ways, all outside the hearing of the jury. (See above forms of offer for the three methods.) The offer must be made at the time of the sustaining of an objection or it will be waived. The theory behind this rule is to provide the trial judge with the most informed opportunity to make the proper ruling.

Original Document Rule
(Best Evidence Rule)

Objection

- *I object to the proponent's offer to show the contents of a writing by the use of secondary evidence.*

Responses

- *The terms of the writing are not directly in issue in the lawsuit and thus the original is not required. The writing is offered to prove* (state reason).

- *The original's absence has been sufficiently accounted for and the secondary evidence is admissible because:*
  - *the original has been shown to have been lost or destroyed,* or
  - *the original cannot be obtained by any available judicial process or procedure,* or
  - *the original is in the possession of an opposing party against whom the contents are offered, that party has failed to produce it, and that party has been put on notice, by pleadings or otherwise, that the contents would be the subject of proof at trial.*

Cross Reference to Federal Rules 1001 through 1008

Explanation

The key to understanding the original document rule is this rule applies where the facts contained in the document are directly in issue in the case and the facts do not exist independent of the document. Typical documents that fall within the rule are written contracts, leases, or wills when the lawsuit is about the existence or interpretation of those documents.

Payment of Medical and Similar Expenses

Objection

- *I object. This evidence is inadmissible as an offer to pay medical expenses.*

Response

- *This statement is admissible because it is not offered on the issue of liability.*

Cross Reference to Federal Rule 409

Explanation

Evidence of offers to pay medical and similar expenses, or payments of the same, are excluded only on the issue of liability and can be offered for any other relevant purpose.

O
P
9

Presumptions

Form of Motion

- *I move for a directed verdict on* (the fact presumed) *because my opponent failed to come forward with sufficient evidence to rebut it.*

Response

- *A directed verdict is inappropriate because we have produced sufficient evidence to rebut the presumption such that a reasonable juror could find for my client on this fact.*

Cross Reference to Federal Rules 301, 302

Explanation

A presumption is a fact which is automatically proved by the proof of some other fact. In all federal-question civil cases, the creation of a presumption forces the opponent to come forward with sufficient evidence to rebut or meet the presumed fact. The presumption does not, however, shift the original burden of proof. Delivery and receipt of information, once it is shown to be have been put in the U. S. mail, with proper address, postage and return address, is a common example of a presumption with the opponent having the ability to offer evidence to rebut the presumption of delivery and receipt.

Privileges

Objection

- *I object to the admission of this evidence on the ground that it is privileged pursuant to* (state the particular form of privilege).

Response

- *This evidence is admissible because:*
  - *it does not fall within the privilege,* or
  - *if privileged, such privilege has been waived.*

Cross Reference to Federal Rule 501

Explanation

The two most commonly encountered privileged communications in federal courts, though by no means the only ones, are the attorney/client privilege and the privileges applicable to spouses.

OPG

Refreshing Present Recollection

Objections

- *I object to the attempt to refresh the witness's recollection in the absence of a demonstrated failure of memory.*

- *I object to the witness's reading from the exhibit used to refresh his or her recollection because it is not in evidence and because it is hearsay.*

Responses

- *The witness has shown a failure of memory and I am attempting to refresh his or her recollection pursuant to Rule 612.*

- *The exhibit used to refresh the witness's recollection is already in evidence and it is either:*
  - *not hearsay,* or
  - *the exhibit meets an exception to the hearsay rule.*

Cross Reference to Federal Rule 612

Explanation

The steps in refreshing a witness's memory are as follows:

R
S

(1) Establish the witness's failure of memory (full or partial).

(2) Mark the refreshing document for identification.

(3) Show the witness the refreshing document and ask the witness to read it silently.

(4) Ask if the witness has read it.

(5) Ask if the witness's memory is refreshed with respect to the forgotten fact.

(6) Take the refreshing exhibit from the witness.

(7) Re-ask the question which drew the original failure of memory.

Relevance:
Generally

Objections

- *I object on the ground that the question calls for an irrelevant answer.*

- *I move to strike the answer as irrelevant.*

Response

- *The evidence is relevant because it has some tendency to make more likely a fact which is material to either a claim or defense in the lawsuit or bears on the weight or credibility of the evidence.*

Cross Reference to Federal Rules 401 and 402

Explanation

Often, the terms "relevance" and "materiality" are used interchangeably. This is incorrect. Materiality has a more precise meaning than relevance and can be seen as being a term which is within the meaning of relevance. Materiality is the relationship between the proposition for which the evidence is offered and the issues in the case. If the evidence is offered to prove a proposition which is

R
S

not a matter in issue, the evidence is said to be immaterial. Relevancy includes both the test of materiality and something more. Relevancy is the tendency of the evidence in question to establish a material proposition.

Relevance: Conditional Admissibility

Objections

- *I object. The proffered evidence is not relevant and admissible unless other facts are proved.*

- *I move to strike the conditionally admitted evidence of* (insert name of witness or evidence). *Counsel has failed to prove additional facts that are necessary to show the relevance of that conditionally admitted evidence.*

Responses

- *I will show the relevance of the proffered evidence by proof of the following additional facts through the testimony of* (insert name of witness).

- *The relevance of the conditionally admitted facts has been shown through the additional evidence given in the testimony of* (insert name of witness).

Cross Reference to Federal Rule 104(b)

Explanation

The judge is given a great deal of authority in making the preliminary findings necessary to determining the admissibility of evidence.

R
S

Relevance:
Exclusion of Relevant Evidence on Grounds of Prejudice, Confusion, or Waste of Time

Objections

- *I object on the ground that this evidence is inadmissible because its probative value is substantially outweighed by the prejudicial effect of the evidence.*

- *The introduction of this evidence will confuse the issue before the jury.*

- *The evidence is merely cumulative.*

Responses

- *The evidence is admissible because it is logically relevant under Rule 401 and:*
  - *its probative value is not substantially outweighed by the danger of unfair prejudice, or*
  - *any potential confusion of issues is easily cured by an instruction by the court, or*
  - *the evidence is corroborative of an issue central to the case.*

R
S

Cross Reference to Federal Rule 403

Explanation

The balancing test of Rules 401 and 403 is tilted heavily in favor of the admissibility of logically relevant evidence or evidence with probative value, in that the prejudice must substantially outweigh the probative value in order to require exclusion.

R
S

Relevance:
Limited Admissibility

Objections

- *I object. The question calls for irrelevant information on the issue* (insert the issue).

- *I object. I move the court instruct the jury that the answer is irrelevant and inadmissible on the issue* (insert the issue) *and I request a limiting instruction.*

- *I object. The question calls for irrelevant information as against my client.*

- *I object. I move the court instruct the jury the answer is irrelevant and admissible as to my client and I request a limiting instruction.*

Responses

- *The evidence offered is relevant and admissible for all purposes and a limiting instruction is inappropriate.*

- *The evidence is relevant and admissible against all parties and a limiting instruction is inappropriate.*

R

S

Cross Reference to Federal Rule 105

Explanation

It is incumbent upon opposing counsel to seek limitation of the evidence to its proper admissible purpose and to request a limiting instruction by the judge. Failure to do so will allow consideration of the evidence for all purposes.

Relevance:
Rule of Completeness

Objections

- *I object to the admissibility of the proffered writing (or recording) unless other portions of the writing (or recording) are also admitted. These other portions are necessary to explain or to put in context the proffered writing (or recording).*

- *I object to the admissibility of the proffered writing (or recording) unless other related writings (or recordings) are also admitted. These other writings (or recordings) are necessary to explain (or to put in context) the proffered writing (or recording).*

Response

- *The proffered statement (or recording) does not need explanation or context. Other portions of the statement (or recording), or additional writings (or recordings), are not necessary to a fair understanding of the proffered statement (or recording).*

Cross Reference to Federal Rule 106

R
S

Explanation

The rule of completeness embodied in Rule 106 is essentially a rule of fairness. Because the appearance of unfairness can seriously damage the credibility of the proponent, the rule of completeness should be anticipated by proffering counsel and every effort should be made to fairly show the appropriate context in which an offered statement or recording was made.

Subsequent Remedial Measures

Objection

- *I object. This is evidence of a subsequent remedial measure.*

Responses

- *This evidence is not offered on the issue of negligence or culpable conduct, but is offered to show:*
  - *notice,*
  - *ownership,*
  - *control,*
  - *feasibility of precautionary measures,* or
  - *impeachment.*
- *My opponent has "opened the door" to this evidence by:*
  - *its pleadings* or
  - *the questioning of* (insert name of witness).

Cross Reference to Federal Rule 407

Explanation

The reason for the evidentiary prohibition against subsequent remedial measures is to create an incentive for correction of defective conditions. Such evidence is *per se* inadmissible only on the issues of negligence or culpable conduct. The 1997 amendment to the rule makes clear that the rule applies to products liability causes of action.

R

S

Federal Rules of Evidence

for United States Courts
and Magistrates

Approved January 2, 1975
Effective July 1, 1975
as Amended to
December 1, 2006

Table of Contents

ARTICLE I
General Provisions

Rule 101 — Scope

These rules govern proceedings in the courts of the United States and before United States bankruptcy judges and United States magistrate judges, to the extent and with the exceptions stated in rule 1101.

Rule 102 — Purpose and Construction

These rules shall be construed to secure fairness in administration, elimination of unjustifiable expense and delay, and promotion of growth and development of the law of evidence to the end that the truth may be ascertained and proceedings justly determined.

Rule 103 — Rulings on Evidence

(a) Effect of erroneous ruling. Error may not be predicated upon a ruling which admits or excludes evidence unless a substantial right of the party is affected, and

(1) Objection. In case the ruling is one admitting evidence, a timely objection or motion to strike appears of record, stating the specific ground of objection, if the specific ground was not apparent from the context; or

(2) Offer of proof. In case the ruling is one excluding evidence, the substance of the evidence was made known to the court by offer or was apparent from the context within which questions were asked.

Once the court makes a definitive ruling on the record admitting or excluding evidence, either at or before trial, a party need not renew an objection or offer of proof to preserve a claim of error for appeal.

(b) Record of offer and ruling. The court may add any other or further statement which shows the character of the evidence, the form in which it was offered, the objection made, and the ruling thereon. It may direct the making of an offer in question and answer form.

(c) Hearing of jury. In jury cases, proceedings shall be conducted, to the extent practicable, so as to prevent inadmissible evidence from being suggested to the jury by any means, such as making statements or offers of proof or asking questions in the hearing of the jury.

(d) Plain error. Nothing in this rule precludes taking notice of plain errors affecting substantial rights although they were not brought to the attention of the court.

Rule 104 — Preliminary Questions

(a) Questions of admissibility generally. Preliminary questions concerning the qualification of a person to be a witness, the existence of a privilege, or the admissibility of evidence shall be determined by the court, subject to the provisions of subdivision (b). In making its determination it is not bound by the rules of evidence except those with respect to privileges.

(b) Relevancy conditioned on fact. When the relevancy of evidence depends upon the fulfillment of a condition of fact, the court shall admit it upon, or subject to, the introduction of evidence sufficient to support a finding of the fulfillment of the condition.

(c) Hearing of jury. Hearings on the admissibility of confessions shall in all cases be conducted out of the hearing of the jury. Hearings on other preliminary matters shall be so conducted when the interests of justice require, or when an accused is a witness and so requests.

(d) Testimony by accused. The accused does not, by testifying upon a preliminary matter, become subject to cross-examination as to other issues in the case.

(e) Weight and credibility. This rule does not limit the right of a party to introduce before the jury evidence relevant to weight or credibility.

Rule 105 — Limited Admissibility

When evidence which is admissible as to one party or for one purpose but not admissible as to another party or for another purpose is admitted, the court, upon request, shall restrict the evidence to its proper scope and instruct the jury accordingly.

Rule 106 — Remainder of or Related Writings or Recorded Statements

When a writing or recorded statement or part thereof is introduced by a party, an adverse party may require the introduction at that time of any other part or any other writing or recorded statement which ought in fairness to be considered contemporaneously with it.

ARTICLE II
Judicial Notice

Rule 201 — Judicial Notice of Adjudicative Facts

(a) Scope of rule. This rule governs only judicial notice of adjudicative facts.

(b) Kinds of facts. A judicially noticed fact must be one not subject to reasonable dispute in that it is either (1) generally known within the territorial jurisdiction of the trial court or (2) capable of accurate and ready determination by resort to sources whose accuracy cannot reasonably be questioned.

(c) When discretionary. A court may take judicial notice, whether requested or not.

(d) When mandatory. A court shall take judicial notice if requested by a party and supplied with the necessary information.

(e) Opportunity to be heard. A party is entitled upon timely request to an opportunity to be heard as to the propriety of taking judicial notice and the tenor of the matter noticed. In the absence of prior notification, the request may be made after judicial notice has been taken.

(f) Time of taking notice. Judicial notice may be taken at any stage of the proceeding.

(g) Instructing jury. In a civil action or proceeding, the court shall instruct the jury to accept as conclusive any fact judicially noticed. In a criminal case, the court shall instruct the jury that it may, but is not required to, accept as conclusive any fact judicially noticed.

ARTICLE III
Presumptions in Civil Actions and Proceedings

Rule 301 — Presumptions in General in Civil Actions and Proceedings

In all civil actions and proceedings not otherwise provided for by Act of Congress or by these rules, a presumption imposes on the party against whom it is directed the burden of going forward with evidence to rebut or meet the presumption, but does not shift to such party the burden of proof in the sense of the risk of nonpersuasion, which remains throughout the trial upon the party on whom it was originally cast.

Rule 302 — Applicability of State Law in Civil Actions and Proceedings

In civil actions and proceedings, the effect of a presumption respecting a fact which is an element of a claim or defense as to which State law supplies the rule of decision is determined in accordance with State law.

ARTICLE IV
Relevancy and Its Limits

Rule 401 — Definition of "Relevant Evidence"

"Relevant evidence" means evidence having any tendency to make the existence of any fact that is of consequence to the determination of the action more probable or less probable than it would be without the evidence.

Rule 402 — Relevant Evidence Generally Admissible; Irrelevant Evidence Inadmissible

All relevant evidence is admissible, except as otherwise provided by the Constitution of the United States, by Act of Congress, by these rules, or by other rules prescribed by the Supreme Court pursuant to statutory authority. Evidence which is not relevant is not admissible.

Rule 403 — Exclusion of Relevant Evidence on Grounds of Prejudice, Confusion, or Waste of Time

Although relevant, evidence may be excluded if its probative value is substantially outweighed by the danger of unfair prejudice, confusion of the issues, or misleading the jury, or by considerations of undue delay, waste of time, or needless presentation of cumulative evidence.

Rule 404 — Character Evidence Not Admissible to Prove Conduct; Exceptions; Other Crimes

(a) Character evidence generally. Evidence of a person's character or a trait of character is not admissible for the purpose of proving action in conformity therewith on a particular occasion, except:

(1) Character of accused. In a criminal case, evidence of a pertinent trait of character offered by an accused, or by the prosecution to rebut the same, or if evidence of a trait of character of the alleged victim of the crime is offered by an accused and admitted under Rule 404(a)(2), evidence of the same trait of character of the accused offered by the prosecution;

(2) Character of alleged victim. In a criminal case, and subject to the limitations imposed by Rule 412, evidence of a pertinent trait of character of the alleged victim of the crime offered by an accused, or by the prosecution to rebut the same, or evidence of a character trait of peacefulness of the alleged victim offered by the prosecution in a homicide case to rebut evidence that the alleged victim was the first aggressor;

(3) Character of witness. Evidence of the character of a witness, as provided in rules 607, 608, and 609.

(b) Other crimes, wrongs, or acts. Evidence of other crimes, wrongs, or acts is not admissible to prove the character of a person in order to show action in conformity therewith. It may, however, be admissible for other purposes, such as proof of motive, opportunity, intent, preparation, plan, knowledge, identity, or absence of mistake or accident, provided that upon request by the accused, the prosecution in a criminal case shall provide reasonable notice in advance of trial, or during trial if the court excuses pretrial notice on good cause shown, of the general nature of any such evidence it intends to introduce at trial.

Rule 405 — Methods of Proving Character

(a) Reputation or opinion. In all cases in which evidence of character or a trait of character of a person is admissible, proof may be made by testimony as to reputation or by testimony in the form of an opinion. On cross-examination, inquiry is allowable into relevant specific instances of conduct.

(b) Specific instances of conduct. In cases in which character or a trait of character of a person is an essential element of a charge, claim, or defense, proof may also be made of specific instances of that person's conduct.

Rule 406 — Habit; Routine Practice

Evidence of the habit of a person or of the routine practice of an organization, whether corroborated or not and regardless of the presence of eyewitnesses, is relevant to prove that the conduct of the person or organization on a particular occasion was in conformity with the habit or routine practice.

Rule 407 — Subsequent Remedial Measures

When, after an injury or harm allegedly caused by an event, measures are taken that, if taken previously, would have made the injury or harm less likely to occur, evidence of the subsequent measures is not admissible to prove negligence, culpable conduct, a defect in a product, a defect in a product's design, or a need for a warning or instruction. This rule does not require the exclusion of evidence of subsequent measures when offered for another purpose, such as proving ownership, control, or feasibility of precautionary measures, if controverted, or impeachment.

Rule 408 — Compromise and Offers to Compromise

(a) Prohibited uses. Evidence of the following is not admissible on behalf of any party, when offered to prove liability for, invalidity of, or amount of a claim that was disputed as to validity or amount, or to impeach through a prior inconsistent statement or contradiction:

(1) furnishing or offering or promising to furnish or accepting or offering or promising to accept a valuable consideration in compromising or attempting to compromise the claim; and

(2) conduct or statements made in compromise negotiations regarding the claim, except when offered in a criminal case and the negotiations related to a claim by a public office or agency in the exercise of regulatory, investigative, or enforcement authority.

(b) Permitted uses. This rule does not require exclusion if the evidence is offered for purposes not prohibited by subdivision (a). Examples of permissible purposes include proving a witness's bias or prejudice, negating a contention of undue delay; and proving an effort to obstruct a criminal investigation or prosecution.

Rule 409 — Payment of Medical and Similar Expenses

Evidence of furnishing or offering or promising to pay medical, hospital, or similar expenses occasioned by an injury is not admissible to prove liability for the injury.

Rule 410 — Inadmissibility of Pleas, Plea Discussions, and Related Statements

Except as otherwise provided in this rule, evidence of the following is not, in any civil or criminal proceeding, admissible against the defendant who made the plea or was a participant in the plea discussions:

> (1) a plea of guilty which was later withdrawn;

> (2) a plea of nolo contendere;

> (3) any statement made in the course of any proceedings under Rule 11 of the Federal Rules of Criminal Procedure or comparable state procedure regarding either of the foregoing pleas; or

> (4) any statement made in the course of plea discussions with an attorney for the prosecuting authority which do not result in a plea of guilty or which result in a plea of guilty later withdrawn.

However, such a statement is admissible (i) in any proceeding wherein another statement made in the course of the same plea or plea discussions has been introduced and the statement ought in fairness be considered contemporaneously with it, or (ii) in a criminal proceeding for perjury or false statement if the statement was made by the defendant under oath, on the record and in the presence of counsel.

Rule 411 — Liability Insurance

Evidence that a person was or was not insured against liability is not admissible upon the issue whether the person acted negligently or otherwise wrongfully. This rule does not require the exclusion of evidence of insurance against liability when offered for another purpose, such as proof of agency, ownership, or control, or bias or prejudice of a witness.

Rule 412 — Sex Offense Cases; Relevance of Victim's Past Sexual Behavior or Alleged Sexual Predisposition

(a) Evidence generally inadmissible. The following evidence is not admissible in any civil or criminal proceeding involving alleged sexual misconduct except as provided in subdivisions (b) and (c):

(1) Evidence offered to prove that any alleged victim engaged in other sexual behavior.

(2) Evidence offered to prove any alleged victim's sexual predisposition.

(b) Exceptions.

(1) In a criminal case, the following evidence is admissible, if otherwise admissible under these rules:

(A) evidence of specific instances of sexual behavior by the alleged victim offered to prove that a person other than the accused was the source of semen, injury or other physical evidence;

(B) evidence of specific instances of sexual behavior by the alleged victim with respect to the person accused of the sexual misconduct offered by the accused to prove consent or by the prosecution; and

(C) evidence the exclusion of which would violate the constitutional rights of the defendant.

(2) In a civil case, evidence offered to prove the sexual behavior or sexual predisposition of any alleged victim is admissible if it is otherwise admissible under these rules and its probative value substantially outweighs the danger of harm to any victim and of unfair prejudice to any party. Evidence of an alleged victim's reputation is admissible only if it has been placed in controversy by the alleged victim.

(c) Procedure to determine admissibility.

(1) A party intending to offer evidence under subdivision (b) must

(A) file a written motion at least 14 days before trial specifically describing the evidence and stating the purpose for which it is offered unless the court, for good cause requires a different time for filing or permits filing during trial; and

(B) serve the motion on all parties and notify the alleged victim or, when appropriate, the alleged victim's guardian or representative.

(2) Before admitting evidence under this rule the court must conduct a hearing in camera and afford the victim and parties a right to attend and be heard. The motion, related papers, and the record of the hearing must be sealed and remain under seal unless the court orders otherwise.

Rule 413 — Evidence of Similar Crimes in Sexual Assault Cases

(a) In a criminal case in which the defendant is accused of an offense of sexual assault, evidence of the defendant's commission of another offense or offenses of sexual assault is admissible, and may be considered for its bearing on any matter to which it is relevant.

(b) In a case in which the Government intends to offer evidence under this rule, the attorney for the Government shall disclose the evidence to the defendant, including statements of witnesses or a summary of the substance of any testimony that is expected to be offered, at least fifteen days before the scheduled date of trial or at such later time as the court may allow for good cause.

(c) This rule shall not be construed to limit the admission or consideration of evidence under any other rule.

(d) For purposes of this rule and Rule 415, "offense of sexual assault" means a crime under Federal law or the law of a State (as defined in section 513 of title 18, United States Code) that involved—

(1) any conduct proscribed by chapter 109A of title 18, United States Code;

(2) contact, without consent, between any part of the defendant's body or an object and the genitals or anus of another person:

(3) contact, without consent, between the genitals or anus of the defendant and any part of another person's body;

(4) deriving sexual pleasure or gratification from the infliction of death, bodily injury, or physical pain on another person; or

(5) an attempt or conspiracy to engage in conduct described in paragraphs (1)-(4).

Rule 414 — Evidence of Similar Crimes in Child Molestation Cases

(a) In a criminal case in which the defendant is accused of an offense of child molestation, evidence of the defendant's commission of another offense or offenses of child molestation is admissible, and may be considered for its bearing on any matter to which it is relevant.

(b) In a case in which the Government intends to offer evidence under this rule, the attorney for the Government shall disclose the evidence to the defendant, including statements of witnesses or a summary of the substance of any testimony that is expected to be offered, at least fifteen days before the scheduled date of trial or at such later time as the court may allow for good cause.

(c) This rule shall not be construed to limit the admission or consideration of evidence under any other rule.

(d) For purposes of this rule and Rule 415, "child" means a person below the age of fourteen, and "offense of child molestation" means a crime under Federal law or the law of a State (as defined in section 513 of title 18, United States Code) that involved—

(1) any conduct proscribed by chapter 109A of title 18, United States Code, that was committed in relation to a child;

(2) any conduct proscribed by chapter 110 of title 18, United States Code;

(3) contact between any part of the defendant's body or an object and the genitals or anus of a child;

(4) contact between the genitals or anus of the defendant and any part of the body of a child;

(5) deriving sexual pleasure or gratification from the infliction of death, bodily injury, or physical pain on a child; or

(6) an attempt or conspiracy to engage in conduct described in paragraphs (1)-(5).

Rule 415 — Evidence of Similar Acts in Civil Cases Concerning Sexual Assault or Child Molestation

(a) In a civil case in which a claim for damages or other relief is predicated on a party's alleged commission of conduct constituting an offense of sexual assault or child molestation, evidence of that party's commission of another offense or offenses of sexual assault or child molestation is admissible and may be considered as provided in Rule 413 and Rule 414 of these rules.

(b) A party who intends to offer evidence under this Rule shall disclose the evidence to the party against whom it will be offered, including statements of witnesses or a summary of the substance of any testimony that is expect to be offered, at least fifteen days before the scheduled date of trial or at such later time as the court may allow for good cause.

(c) This rule shall not be construed to limit the admission or consideration of evidence under any other rule.

ARTICLE V
Privileges

Rule 501 — General Rule

Except as otherwise required by the Constitution of the United States or provided by Act of Congress or in rules prescribed by the Supreme Court pursuant to statutory authority, the privilege of a witness, person, government, State, or political subdivision thereof shall be governed by the principles of the common law as they may be interpreted by the courts of the United States in the light of reason and experience. However, in civil actions and proceedings, with respect to an element of a claim or defense as to which State law supplies the rule of decision, the privilege of a witness, person, government, State, or political subdivision thereof shall be determined in accordance with State law.

ARTICLE VI
Witnesses

Rule 601 — General Rule of Competency

Every person is competent to be a witness except as otherwise provided in these rules. However, in civil actions and proceedings, with respect to an element of a claim or defense as to which State law supplies the rule of decision, the competency of a witness shall be determined in accordance with State law.

Rule 602 — Lack of Personal Knowledge

A witness may not testify to a matter unless evidence is introduced sufficient to support a finding that the witness has personal knowledge of the matter. Evidence to prove personal knowledge may, but need not, consist of the witness' own testimony. This rule is subject to the provisions of rule 703, relating to opinion testimony by expert witnesses.

Rule 603 — Oath or Affirmation

Before testifying, every witness shall be required to declare that the witness will testify truthfully, by oath or affirmation administered in a form calculated to awaken the witness' conscience and impress the witness' mind with the duty to do so.

Rule 604 — Interpreters

An interpreter is subject to the provisions of these rules relating to qualification as an expert and the administration of an oath or affirmation to make a true translation.

Rule 605 — Competency of Judge as Witness

The judge presiding at the trial may not testify in that trial as a witness. No objection need be made in order to preserve the point.

Rule 606 — Competency of Juror as Witness

(a) At the trial. A member of the jury may not testify as a witness before that jury in the trial of the case in which the juror is sitting. If the juror is called so to testify, the opposing party shall be afforded an opportunity to object out of the presence of the jury.

(b) Inquiry into validity of verdict or indictment. Upon an inquiry into the validity of a verdict or indictment, a juror may not testify as to any matter or statement occurring during the course of the jury's deliberations or to the effect of anything upon that or any other juror's mind or emotions as influencing the juror to assent to or dissent from the verdict or indictment or concerning the juror's mental processes in connection therewith. But a juror may testify about (1) whether extraneous prejudicial information was improperly brought to the jury's attention, (2) whether any outside influence was improperly brought to bear upon any juror, or (3) whether there was a mistake in entering the verdict onto the verdict form. A juror's affidavit or evidence of any statement by the juror may not be received on a matter about which the juror would be precluded from testifying.

Rule 607 — Who May Impeach

The credibility of a witness may be attacked by any party, including the party calling the witness.

Rule 608 — Evidence of Character and Conduct of Witness

(a) Opinion and reputation evidence of character. The credibility of a witness may be attacked or supported by evidence in the form of opinion or reputation, but subject to these limitations: (1) the evidence may refer only to character for truthfulness or untruthfulness, and (2) evidence of truthful character is admissible only after the character of the witness for truthfulness has been attacked by opinion or reputation evidence or otherwise.

(b) Specific instances of conduct. Specific instances of the conduct of a witness, for the purpose of attacking or supporting the witness' character for truthfulness, other than conviction of crime as provided in rule 609, may not be proved by extrinsic evidence. They may, however, in the discretion of the court, if probative of truthfulness or untruthfulness, be inquired into on cross-examination of the witness (1) concerning the witness' character for truthfulness or untruthfulness, or (2) concerning the character for truthfulness or untruthfulness of another witness as to which character the witness being cross-examined has testified.

The giving of testimony, whether by an accused or by any other witness, does not operate as a waiver of the accused's or the witness' privilege against self-incrimination when examined with respect to matters that relate only to character for truthfulness.

Rule 609 — Impeachment by Evidence of Conviction of Crime

(a) General rule. For the purpose of attacking the character for truthfulness of a witness,

(1) evidence that a witness other than an accused has been convicted of a crime shall be admitted subject to Rule 403, if the crime was

punishable by death or imprisonment in excess of one year under the law under which the witness was convicted, and evidence that an accused has been convicted of such a crime shall be admitted if the court determines that the probative value of admitting this evidence outweighs its prejudicial effect to the accused; and

(2) evidence that any witness has been convicted of a crime shall be admitted regardless of the punishment, if it readily can be determined that estabishing the elements of the crime required proof or admission of an act of dishonesty or false statement by the witness.

(b) Time limit. Evidence of a conviction under this rule is not admissible if a period of more than ten years has elapsed since the date of the conviction or of the release of the witness from the confinement imposed for that conviction, whichever is the later date, unless the court determines, in the interests of justice, that the probative value of the conviction supported by specific facts and circumstances substantially outweighs its prejudicial effect. However, evidence of a conviction more than 10 years old as calculated herein, is not admissible unless the proponent gives to the adverse party sufficient advance written notice of intent to use such evidence to provide the adverse party with a fair opportunity to contest the use of such evidence.

(c) Effect of pardon, annulment, or certificate of rehabilitation. Evidence of a conviction is not admissible under this rule if (1) the conviction has been the subject of a pardon, annulment, certificate of rehabilitation, or other equivalent procedure based on a finding of the rehabilitation of the person convicted, and that person has not been convicted of a subsequent crime which was punishable by death or imprisonment in excess of one year, or (2) the conviction has been the subject of a pardon, annulment, or other equivalent procedure based on a finding of innocence.

(d) Juvenile adjudications. Evidence of juvenile adjudications is generally not admissible under this rule. The court may, however, in a criminal case allow evidence of a juvenile adjudication of a witness other than the accused if conviction of the offense would be admissible to attack the credibility of an adult and the court is satisfied that admission in evidence is necessary for a fair determination of the issue of guilt or innocence.

(e) Pendency of appeal. The pendency of an appeal therefrom does not render evidence of a conviction inadmissible. Evidence of the pendency of an appeal is admissible.

Rule 610 — Religious Beliefs or Opinions

Evidence of the beliefs or opinions of a witness on matters of religion is not admissible for the purpose of showing that by reason of their nature the witness' credibility is impaired or enhanced.

Rule 611 — Mode and Order of Interrogation and Presentation

(a) Control by court. The court shall exercise reasonable control over the mode and order of interrogating witnesses and presenting evidence so as to (1) make the interrogation and presentation effective for the ascertainment of the truth, (2) avoid needless consumption of time, and (3) protect witnesses from harassment or undue embarrassment.

(b) Scope of cross-examination. Cross-examination should be limited to the subject matter of the direct examination and matters affecting the credibility of the witness. The court may, in the exercise of discretion, permit inquiry into additional matters as if on direct examination.

(c) Leading questions. Leading questions should not be used on the direct examination of a witness except as may be necessary to develop the witness' testimony. Ordinarily leading questions should be permitted on cross-examination. When a party calls a hostile witness, an adverse party, or a witness identified with an adverse party, interrogation may be by leading questions.

Rule 612 — Writing Used to Refresh Memory

Except as otherwise provided in criminal proceedings by section 3500 of title 18, United States Code, if a witness uses a writing to refresh memory for the purpose of testifying, either

(1) while testifying, or

(2) before testifying, if the court in its discretion determines it is necessary in the interests of justice,

an adverse party is entitled to have the writing produced at the hearing, to inspect it, to cross-examine the witness thereon, and to introduce in evidence those portions which relate to the testimony of the witness. If it is claimed that the writing contains matters not related to the subject matter of the testimony the court shall examine the writing in camera, excise any portions not so related, and order delivery of the remainder to the party entitled thereto. Any portion withheld over objections shall be preserved and made available to the appellate court in the event of an appeal. If a writing is not produced or delivered pursuant to order under this rule, the court shall make any order justice requires, except that in criminal cases when the prosecution elects not to comply, the order shall be one striking the testimony or, if the court in its discretion determines that the interests of justice so require, declaring a mistrial.

Rule 613 — Prior Statements of Witnesses

(a) Examining witness concerning prior statement. In examining a witness concerning a prior statement made by the witness, whether written or not, the statement need not be shown nor its contents disclosed to the witness at that time, but on request the same shall be shown or disclosed to opposing counsel.

(b) Extrinsic evidence of prior inconsistent statement of witness. Extrinsic evidence of a prior inconsistent statement by a witness is not admissible unless the witness is afforded an opportunity to explain or deny the same and the opposite party is afforded an opportunity to interrogate the witness thereon, or the interests of justice otherwise require. This provision does not apply to admissions of a party-opponent as defined in rule 801(d)(2).

Rule 614 — Calling and Interrogation of Witnesses by Court

(a) Calling by court. The court may, on its own motion or at the suggestion of a party, call witnesses, and all parties are entitled to cross-examine witnesses thus called.

(b) Interrogation by court. The court may interrogate witnesses, whether called by itself or by a party.

(c) Objections. Objections to the calling of witnesses by the court or to interrogation by it may be made at the time or at the next available opportunity when the jury is not present.

Rule 615 — Exclusion of Witnesses

At the request of a party the court shall order witnesses excluded so that they cannot hear the testimony of other witnesses, and it may make the order of its own motion. This rule does not authorize exclusion of (1) a party who is a natural person, or (2) an officer or employee of a party which is not a natural person designated as its representative by its attorney, or (3) a person whose presence is shown by a party to be essential to the presentation of the party's cause, or (4) a person authorized by statute to be present.

ARTICLE VII
Opinions and Expert Testimony

Rule 701 — Opinion Testimony by Lay Witnesses

If the witness is not testifying as an expert, the witness' testimony in the form of opinions or inferences is limited to those opinions or inferences which are (a) rationally based on the perception of the witness, (b) helpful to a clear understanding of the witness' testimony or the determination of a fact in issue, and (c) not based on scientific, technical, or other specialized knowledge within the scope of Rule 702.

Rule 702 — Testimony by Experts

If scientific, technical, or other specialized knowledge will assist the trier of fact to understand the evidence or to determine a fact in issue, a witness qualified as an expert by knowledge, skill, experience, training, or education, may testify thereto in the form of an opinion or otherwise, if (1) the testimony is based upon sufficient facts or data, (2) the testimony is the product of reliable principles and methods, and (3) the witness has applied the principles and methods reliably to the facts of the case.

Rule 703 — Bases of Opinion Testimony by Experts

The facts or data in the particular case upon which an expert bases an opinion or inference may be those perceived by or made known to the expert at or before the hearing. If of a type reasonably relied upon by experts in the particular field in forming opinions or inferences upon the subject, the facts or data need not be admissible in evidence in order for the opinion or inference to be admitted. Facts or data that are otherwise inadmissible shall not be disclosed to the jury by the proponent of the opinion or inference unless the court determines that their probative value in assisting the jury to evaluate the expert's opinion substantially outweighs their prejudicial effect.

Rule 704 — Opinion on Ultimate Issue

(a) Except as provided in subdivision (b), testimony in the form of an opinion or inference otherwise admissible is not objectionable because it embraces an ultimate issue to be decided by the trier of fact.

(b) No expert witness testifying with respect to the mental state or condition of a defendant in a criminal case may state an opinion or inference as to whether the defendant did or did not have the mental state or condition constituting an element of the crime charged or of a defense thereto. Such ultimate issues are matters for the trier of fact alone.

Rule 705 — Disclosure of Facts or Data Underlying Expert Opinion

The expert may testify in terms of opinion or inference and give reasons therefor without first testifying to the underlying facts or data, unless the court requires otherwise. The expert may in any event be required to disclose the underlying facts or data on cross-examination.

Rule 706 — Court Appointed Experts

(a) Appointment. The court may on its own motion or on the motion of any party enter an order to show cause why expert witnesses should not be appointed, and may request the parties to submit nominations. The court may appoint any expert witnesses agreed upon by the parties, and may appoint expert witnesses of its own selection. An expert witness shall not be appointed by the court unless the witness consents to act. A witness so appointed shall be informed of the witness' duties by the court in writing, a copy of which shall be filed with the clerk, or at a conference in which the parties shall have opportunity to participate. A witness so appointed shall advise the parties of the witness' findings, if any; the witness' deposition may be taken by any party; and the witness may be called to testify by the court or any party. The witness shall be subject to cross-examination by each party, including a party calling the witness.

(b) Compensation. Expert witnesses so appointed are entitled to reasonable compensation in whatever sum the court may allow. The compensation thus fixed is payable from funds which may be provided by law in criminal cases and civil actions and proceedings involving just compensation under the fifth amendment. In other civil actions and proceedings the compensation shall be paid by the parties in such proportion and at such time as the court directs, and thereafter charged in like manner as other costs.

(c) Disclosure of appointment. In the exercise of its discretion, the court may authorize disclosure to the jury of the fact that the court appointed the expert witness.

(d) Parties' experts of own selection. Nothing in this rule limits the parties in calling expert witnesses of their own selection.

ARTICLE VIII
Hearsay

Rule 801 — Definitions

The following definitions apply under this article:

(a) Statement. A "statement" is (1) an oral or written assertion or (2) nonverbal conduct of a person, if it is intended by the person as an assertion.

(b) Declarant. A "declarant" is a person who makes a statement.

(c) Hearsay. "Hearsay" is a statement, other than one made by the declarant while testifying at the trial or hearing, offered in evidence to prove the truth of the matter asserted.

(d) Statements which are not hearsay. A statement is not hearsay if –

(1) Prior statement by witness. The declarant testifies at the trial or hearing and is subject to cross-examination concerning the statement, and the statement is (A) inconsistent with the declarant's testimony, and was given under oath subject to the penalty of perjury at a trial, hearing, or other proceeding, or in a deposition, or (B) consistent with the declarant's testimony and is offered to rebut an express or implied charge against the declarant of recent fabrication or improper influence or motive, or (C) one of identification of a person made after perceiving the person; or

(2) Admission by party-opponent. The statement is offered against a party and is (A) the party's own statement, in either an individual or a representative capacity or (B) a statement of which the party has manifested an adoption or belief in its truth, or (C) a statement by a person authorized by the party to make a statement concerning the subject, or (D) a statement by the party's agent or servant concerning a matter within the scope of the agency or employment, made during the existence of the relationship, or (E) a statement by a coconspirator of a party during the course and in furtherance of the conspiracy. The contents of the statement shall be considered but are not alone sufficient to establish the declarant's authority under subdivision (C), the agency or employment relationship and scope thereof under subdivision (D), or the existence of the conspiracy and the participation therein of the declarant and the party against whom the statement is offered under subdivision (E).

Rule 802 — Hearsay Rule

Hearsay is not admissible except as provided by these rules or by other rules prescribed by the Supreme Court pursuant to statutory authority or by Act of Congress.

Rule 803 — Hearsay Exceptions; Availability of Declarant Immaterial

The following are not excluded by the hearsay rule, even though the declarant is available as a witness:

(1) Present sense impression. A statement describing or explaining an event or condition made while the declarant was perceiving the event or condition, or immediately thereafter.

(2) Excited utterance. A statement relating to a startling event or condition made while the declarant was under the stress of excitement caused by the event or condition.

(3) Then existing mental, emotional, or physical condition. A statement of the declarant's then existing state of mind, emotion, sensation, or physical condition (such as intent, plan, motive, design, mental feeling, pain, and bodily health), but not including a statement of memory or belief to prove the fact remembered or believed unless it relates to the execution, revocation, identification, or terms of declarant's will.

(4) Statements for purposes of medical diagnosis or treatment. Statements made for purposes of medical diagnosis or treatment and describing medical history, or past or present symptoms, pain, or sensations, or the inception or general character of the cause or external source thereof insofar as reasonably pertinent to diagnosis or treatment.

(5) Recorded recollection. A memorandum or record concerning a matter about which a witness once had knowledge but now has insufficient recollection to enable the witness to testify fully and accurately, shown to have been made or adopted by the witness when the matter was fresh in the witness' memory and to reflect that knowledge correctly. If admitted, the memorandum or record may be read into evidence but may not itself be received as an exhibit unless offered by an adverse party.

(6) Records of regularly conducted activity. A memorandum, report, record, or data compilation, in any form, of acts, events, conditions, opinions, or diagnoses, made at or near the time by, or from information transmitted by, a person with knowledge, if kept in the course of a regularly conducted business activity, and if it was the regular practice of that business activity to make the memorandum, report, record, or data compilation, all as shown by the testimony of the custodian or other qualified witness, or by certification that complies with Rule 902(11), Rule 902(12), or a statute permitting certification, unless the source of information or the method or circumstances of preparation indicate lack of trustworthiness. The term "business" as used in this paragraph includes business, institution, association, profession, occupation, and calling of every kind, whether or not conducted for profit.

(7) Absence of entry in records kept in accordance with the provisions of paragraph (6). Evidence that a matter is not included in the memoranda reports, records, or data compilations, in any form, kept in accordance with the provisions of paragraph (6), to prove the nonoccurrence or nonexistence of the matter, if the matter was of a kind of which a memorandum, report, record, or data compilation was regularly made and preserved, unless the sources of information or other circumstances indicate lack of trustworthiness.

(8) Public records and reports. Records, reports, statements, or data compilations, in any form, of public offices or agencies, setting forth (A) the activities of the office or agency, or (B) matters observed pursuant to duty imposed by law as to which matters there was a duty to report, excluding, however, in criminal cases matters observed by police officers and other law enforcement personnel, or (C) in civil actions and proceedings and against the Government in criminal cases, factual findings resulting from an investigation made pursuant to authority granted by law, unless the sources of information or other circumstances indicate lack of trustworthiness.

(9) Records of vital statistics. Records or data compilations, in any form, of births, fetal deaths, deaths, or marriages, if the report thereof was made to a public office pursuant to requirements of law.

(10) Absence of public record or entry. To prove the absence of a record, report, statement, or data compilation, in any form, or the nonoccurrence or nonexistence of a matter of which a record, report, statement, or data compilation, in any form, was regularly made and preserved by a public office or agency, evidence in the form of a certification in accordance with rule 902, or testimony, that diligent search failed to disclose the record, report, statement, or date compilation, or entry.

(11) Records of religious organizations. Statements of births, marriages, divorces, deaths, legitimacy, ancestry, relationship by blood or marriage, or other similar facts of personal or family history, contained in a regularly kept record of a religious organization.

(12) Marriage, baptismal, and similar certificates. Statements of fact contained in a certificate that the maker performed a marriage or other ceremony or administered a sacrament, made by a clergyman, public official, or other person authorized by the rules or practices of a religious organization or by law to perform the act certified, and purporting to have been issued at the time of the act or within a reasonable time thereafter.

(13) Family records. Statements of fact concerning personal or family history contained in family Bibles, genealogies, charts, engravings on rings, inscriptions on family portraits, engravings on urns, crypts, or tombstones, or the like.

(14) Records of documents affecting an interest in property. The record of a document purporting to establish or affect an interest in property, as proof of the content of the original recorded document and its execution and delivery by each person by whom it purports to have been executed, if the record is a record of a public office and an applicable statute authorizes the recording of documents of that kind in that office.

(15) Statements in documents affecting an interest in property. A statement contained in a document purporting to establish or affect an interest in property if the matter stated was relevant to the purpose of the document, unless dealings with the property since the document was made have been inconsistent with the truth of the statement or the purport of the document.

(16) Statements in ancient documents. Statements in a document in existence twenty years or more the authenticity of which is established.

(17) Market reports, commercial publications. Market quotations, tabulations, lists, directories, or other published compilations, generally used and relied upon by the public or by persons in particular occupations.

(18) Learned treatises. To the extent called to the attention of an expert witness upon cross-examination or relied upon by the expert witness in direct examination, statements contained in published treatises, periodicals, or pamphlets on a subject of history, medicine, or other science or art, established as a reliable authority by the testimony or admission of the witness or by other expert testimony or by judicial notice. If admitted, the statements may be read into evidence but may not be received as exhibits.

(19) Reputation concerning personal or family history. Reputation among members of a person's family by blood, adoption, or marriage, or among a person's associates, or in the community, concerning a person's birth, adoption, marriage, divorce, death, legitimacy, relationship by blood, adoption, or marriage, ancestry, or other similar fact of personal or family history.

(20) Reputation concerning boundaries or general history. Reputation in a community, arising before the controversy, as to boundaries of or customs affecting lands in the community, and reputation as to events of general history important to the community or State or nation in which located.

(21) Reputation as to character. Reputation of a person's character among associates or in the community.

(22) Judgment of previous conviction. Evidence of a final judgment, entered after a trial or upon a plea of guilty (but not upon a plea of nolo contendere), adjudging a person guilty of a crime punishable by death or imprisonment in excess of one year, to prove any fact essential to sustain the judgment, but not including, when offered by the Government in a criminal prosecution for purposes other than impeachment, judgments against persons other than the accused. The pendency of an appeal may be shown but does not affect admissibility.

(23) Judgment as to personal, family or general history, or boundaries. Judgments as proof of matters of personal, family or general history, or boundaries, essential to the judgment, if the same would be provable by evidence of reputation.

(24) [Transferred to Rule 807]

Rule 804 — Hearsay Exceptions; Declarant Unavailable

(a) Definition of unavailability. "Unavailability as a witness" includes situations in which the declarant–

(1) is exempted by ruling of the court on the ground of privilege from testifying concerning the subject matter of the declarant's statement; or

(2) persists in refusing to testify concerning the subject matter of the declarant's statement despite an order of the court to do so; or

(3) testifies to a lack of memory of the subject matter of the declarant's statement; or

(4) is unable to be present or to testify at the hearing because of death or then existing physical or mental illness or infirmity; or

(5) is absent from the hearing and the proponent of a statement has been unable to procure the declarant's attendance (or in the case of a hearsay exception under subdivisions (b)(2), (3), or (4), the declarant's attendance or testimony) by process or other reasonable means.

A declarant is not unavailable as a witness if exemption, refusal, claim of lack of memory, inability, or absence is due to the procurement or wrongdoing of the proponent of a statement for the purpose of preventing the witness from attending or testifying.

(b) Hearsay exceptions. The following are not excluded by the hearsay rule if the declarant is unavailable as a witness:

(1) Former testimony. Testimony given as a witness at another hearing of the same or a different proceeding, or in a deposition taken in compliance with law in the course of the same or another proceeding, if the party against whom the testimony is now offered, or, in a civil action or proceeding, a predecessor in interest, had an opportunity and similar motive to develop the testimony by direct, cross, or redirect examination.

(2) Statement under belief of impending death. In a prosecution for homicide or in a civil action or proceeding, a statement made by a declarant while believing that the declarant's death was imminent, concerning the cause or circumstances of what the declarant believed to be impending death.

(3) Statement against interest. A statement which was at the time of its making so far contrary to the declarant's pecuniary or proprietary interest, or so far tended to subject the declarant to civil or criminal liability, or to render invalid a claim by the declarant against another, that a reasonable person in the declarant's position would not have made the statement unless believing it to be true. A statement tending to expose the declarant to criminal liability and offered to exculpate the accused is not admissible unless corroborating circumstances clearly indicate the trustworthiness of the statement.

(4) Statement of personal or family history. (A) A statement concerning the declarant's own birth, adoption, marriage, divorce, legitimacy, relationship by blood, adoption, or marriage, ancestry, or other similar fact of personal or family history, even though declarant had no means of acquiring personal knowledge of the matter stated; or (B) a statement concerning the foregoing matters, and death also, of another person, if the declarant was related to the other by blood, adoption, or marriage or was so intimately associated with the other's family as to be likely to have accurate information concerning the matter declared.

(5) [Transferred to Rule 807]

(6) Forfeiture by wrongdoing. A statement offered against a party that has engaged or acquiesced in wrongdoing that was intended to, and did, procure the unavailability of the declarant as a witness.

Rule 805 — Hearsay Within Hearsay

Hearsay included within hearsay is not excluded under the hearsay rule if each part of the combined statements conforms with an exception to the hearsay rule provided in these rules.

Rule 806 — Attacking and Supporting Credibility of Declarant

When a hearsay statement, or a statement defined in Rule 801(d)(2)(C), (D), or (E), has been admitted in evidence, the credibility of the declarant may be attacked, and if attacked may be supported, by any evidence which would be admissible for those purposes if declarant had testified as a witness. Evidence of a statement or conduct by the declarant at any time, inconsistent with the declarant's hearsay statement, is not subject to any requirement that the declarant may have been afforded an opportunity to deny or explain. If the party against whom a hearsay statement has been admitted calls the declarant as a witness, the party is entitled to examine the declarant on the statement as if under cross-examination.

Rule 807 — Residual Exception

A statement not specifically covered by Rule 803 or 804 but having equivalent circumstantial guarantees of trustworthiness, is not excluded by the hearsay rule, if the court determines that (A) the statement is offered as evidence of a material fact; (B) the statement is more probative on the point for which it is offered than any other evidence which the proponent can procure through reasonable efforts; and (C) the general purposes of these rules and the interests of justice will best be served by admission of the statement into evidence. However, a statement may not be admitted under this exception unless the proponent of it makes known to the adverse party sufficiently in advance of the trial or hearing to provide the adverse party with a fair opportunity to prepare to meet it, the proponent's intention to offer the statement and the particulars of it, including the name and address of the declarant.

ARTICLE IX
Authentication and Identification

Rule 901 — Requirement of Authentication or Identification

(a) **General provision.** The requirement of authentication or identification as a condition precedent to admissibility is satisfied by evidence sufficient to support a finding that the matter in question is what its proponent claims.

(b) Illustrations. By way of illustration only, and not by way of limitation, the following are examples of authentication or identification conforming with the requirements of this rule:

(1) Testimony of witness with knowledge. Testimony that a matter is what it is claimed to be.

(2) Nonexpert opinion on handwriting. Nonexpert opinion as to the genuineness of handwriting, based upon familiarity not acquired for purposes of litigation.

(3) Comparison by trier or expert witness. Comparison by the trier of fact or by expert witnesses with specimens which have been authenticated.

(4) Distinctive characteristics and the like. Appearance, contents, substance, internal patterns, or other distinctive characteristics, taken in conjunction with circumstances.

(5) Voice identification. Identification of a voice, whether heard firsthand or through mechanical or electronic transmission or recording, by opinion based upon hearing the voice at any time under circumstances connecting it with the alleged speaker.

(6) Telephone conversations. Telephone conversations, by evidence that a call was made to the number assigned at the time by the telephone company to a particular person or business, if (A) in the case of a person, circumstances, including self-identification, show the person answering to be the one called, or (B) in the case of a business, the call was made to a place of business and the conversation related to business reasonably transacted over the telephone.

(7) Public records or reports. Evidence that a writing authorized by law to be recorded or filed and in fact recorded or filed in a public office, or a purported public record, report, statement, or data compilation, in any form, is from the public office where items of this nature are kept.

(8) Ancient documents or data compilation. Evidence that a document or data compilation, in any form, (A) is in such condition as to create no suspicion concerning its authenticity, (B) was in a place where it, if authentic, would likely be, and (C) has been in existence 20 years or more at the time it is offered.

(9) Process or system. Evidence describing a process or system used to produce a result and showing that the process or system produces an accurate result.

(10) Methods provided by statute or rule. Any method of authentication or identification provided by Act of Congress or by other rules prescribed by the Supreme Court pursuant to statutory authority.

Rule 902 — Self-Authentication

Extrinsic evidence of authenticity as a condition precedent to admissibility is not required with respect to the following:

(1) Domestic public documents under seal. A document bearing a seal purporting to be that of the United States, or of any State, district, Commonwealth, territory, or insular possession thereof, or the Panama Canal Zone, or the Trust Territory of the Pacific Islands, or of a political subdivision, department, officer, or agency thereof, and a signature purporting to be an attestation or execution.

(2) Domestic public documents not under seal. A document purporting to bear the signature in the official capacity of an officer or employee of any entity included in paragraph (1) hereof, having no seal, if a public officer having a seal and having official duties in the district or political subdivision of the officer or employee certifies under seal that the signer has the official capacity and that the signature is genuine.

(3) Foreign public documents. A document purporting to be executed or attested in an official capacity by a person authorized by the laws of a foreign country to make the execution or attestation, and accompanied by a final certification as to the genuineness of the signature and official position (A) of the executing or attesting person, or (B) of any foreign official whose certificate of genuineness of signature and official position relates to the execution or attestation or is in a chain of certificates of genuineness of signature and official position relating to the execution or attestation. A final certification may be made by a secretary of embassy or legation, consul general, consul, vice consul, or consular agent of the United States, or a diplomatic or consular official of the foreign country assigned or accredited to the United States. If reasonable opportunity has been given to all parties to investigate the authenticity and accuracy of official documents, the court may, for good cause shown, order that they be treated as presumptively authentic without final certification or permit them to be evidenced by an attested summary with or without final certification.

(4) Certified copies of public records. A copy of an official record or report or entry therein, or of a document authorized by law to be recorded or filed and actually recorded or filed in a public office, including data compilations in any form, certified as correct by the custodian or other person authorized to make the certification, by certificate complying with paragraph (1), (2), or (3) of this rule or complying with any Act of Congress or rule prescribed by the Supreme Court pursuant to statutory authority.

(5) Official publications. Books, pamphlets, or other publications purporting to be issued by public authority.

(6) Newspapers and periodicals. Printed materials purporting to be newspapers or periodicals.

(7) Trade inscriptions and the like. Inscriptions, signs, tags, or labels purporting to have been affixed in the course of business and indicating ownership, control, or origin.

(8) Acknowledged documents. Documents accompanied by a certificate of acknowledgment executed in the manner provided by law by a notary public or other officer authorized by law to take acknowledgments.

(9) Commercial paper and related documents. Commercial paper, signatures thereon, and documents relating thereto to the extent provided by general commercial law.

(10) Presumptions under Acts of Congress. Any signature, document or other matter declared by Act of Congress to be presumptively or prima facie genuine or authentic.

(11) Certified domestic records of regularly conducted activity. The original or a duplicate of a domestic record of regularly conducted activity that would be admissible under Rule 803(6) if accompanied by a written declaration of its custodian or other qualified person, in a manner complying with any Act of Congress or rule prescribed by the Supreme Court pursuant to statutory authority, certifying that the record—

(A) was made at or near the time of the occurrence of the matters set forth by, or from information transmitted by, a person with knowledge of those matters;

(B) was kept in the course of the regularly conducted activity; and

(C) was made by the regularly conducted activity as a regular practice.

A party intending to offer a record into evidence under this paragraph must provide written notice of that intention to all adverse parties, and must make the record and declaration available for inspection sufficiently in advance of their offer into evidence to provide an adverse party with a fair opportunity to challenge them.

(12) Certified foreign records of regularly conducted activity. In a civil case, the original or a duplicate of a foreign record of regularly conducted activity that would be admissible under Rule 803(6) if accompanied by a written declaration by its custodian or other qualified person certifying that the record—

(A) was made at or near the time of the occurrence of the matters set forth by, or from information transmitted by, a person with knowledge of those matters;

(B) was kept in the course of the regularly conducted activity; and

(C) was made by the regularly conducted activity as a regular practice.

The declaration must be signed in a manner that, if falsely made, would subject the maker to criminal penalty under the laws of the country where the declaration is signed. A party intending to offer a record into evidence under this paragraph must provide written notice of that intention to all adverse parties, and must make the record and declaration available for inspection sufficiently in advance of their offer into evidence to provide an adverse party with a fair opportunity to challenge them.

Rule 903 — Subscribing Witness' Testimony Unnecessary

The testimony of a subscribing witness is not necessary to authenticate a writing unless required by the laws of the jurisdiction whose laws govern the validity of the writing.

A R T I C L E X
Contents of Writings, Recordings, and Photographs

Rule 1001 — Definitions

For purposes of this article the following definitions are applicable:

(1) **Writings and recordings.** "Writings" and "recordings" consist of letters, words, or numbers, or their equivalent, set down by handwriting, typewriting, printing, photostating, photographing, magnetic impulse, mechanical or electronic recording, or other form of data compilation.

(2) **Photographs.** "Photographs" include still photographs, X-ray films, videotapes, and motion pictures.

(3) Original. An "original" of a writing or recording is the writing or recording itself or any counterpart intended to have the same effect by a person executing or issuing it. An "original" of a photograph includes the negative or any print therefrom. If data are stored in a computer or similar device, any printout or other output readable by sight, shown to reflect the data accurately, is an "original."

(4) Duplicate. A "duplicate" is a counterpart produced by the same impression as the original, or from the same matrix, or by means of photography, including enlargements and miniatures, or by mechanical or electronic re-recording, or by chemical reproduction, or by other equivalent techniques which accurately reproduces the original.

Rule 1002 — Requirement of Original

To prove the content of a writing, recording, or photograph, the original writing, recording, or photograph is required, except as otherwise provided in these rules or by Act of Congress.

Rule 1003 — Admissibility of Duplicates

A duplicate is admissible to the same extent as an original unless (1) a genuine question is raised as to the authenticity of the original or (2) in the circumstances it would be unfair to admit the duplicate in lieu of the original.

Rule 1004 — Admissibility of Other Evidence of Contents

The original is not required, and other evidence of the contents of a writing, recording, or photograph is admissible if –

(1) Originals lost or destroyed. All originals are lost or have been destroyed, unless the proponent lost or destroyed them in bad faith; or

(2) Original not obtainable. No original can be obtained by any available judicial process or procedure; or

(3) Original in possession of opponent. At a time when an original was under the control of the party against whom offered, that party was put on notice, by the pleadings or otherwise, that the contents would be a subject of proof at the hearing, and that party does not produce the original at the hearing; or

(4) Collateral matters. The writing, recording, or photograph is not closely related to a controlling issue.

Rule 1005 — Public Records

The contents of an official record, or of a document authorized to be recorded or filed and actually recorded or filed, including data compilations in any form, if otherwise admissible, may be proved by copy, certified as correct in accordance with rule 902 or testified to be correct by a witness who has compared it with the original. If a copy which complies with the foregoing cannot be obtained by the exercise of reasonable diligence, then other evidence of the contents may be given.

Rule 1006 — Summaries

The contents of voluminous writings, recordings, or photographs which cannot conveniently be examined in court may be presented in the form of a chart, summary, or calculation. The originals, or duplicates, shall be made available for examination or copying, or both, by other parties at reasonable time and place. The court may order that they be produced in court.

Rule 1007 — Testimony or Written Admission of Party

Contents of writings, recordings, or photographs may be proved by the testimony or deposition of the party against whom offered or by that party's written admission, without accounting for the nonproduction of the original.

Rule 1008 — Functions of Court and Jury

When the admissibility of other evidence of contents of writings, recordings, or photographs under these rules depends upon the fulfillment of a condition of fact, the question whether the condition has been fulfilled is ordinarily for the court to determine in accordance with the provisions of rule 104. However, when an issue is raised (a) whether the asserted writing ever existed, or (b) whether another writing, recording, or photograph produced at the trial is the original, or (c) whether other evidence of contents correctly reflects the contents, the issue is for the trier of fact to determine as in the case of other issues of fact.

ARTICLE XI
Miscellaneous Rules

Rule 1101 — Applicability of Rules

(a) Courts and judges. These rules apply to the United States district courts, the District Court of Guam, the District Court of the Virgin Islands, the District Court for the Northern Mariana Islands, the United States Courts of Appeals, the United States Claims Court, and to United States bankruptcy judges and United States magistrate judges, in the actions, cases, and proceedings and to the extent hereinafter set forth. The terms "judge" and "court" in these rules include United States bankruptcy judges and United States magistrate judges.

(b) Proceedings generally. These rules apply generally to civil actions and proceedings, including admiralty and maritime cases, to criminal cases and proceedings, to contempt proceedings except those in which the court may act summarily, and to proceedings and cases under title 11, United States Code.

(c) Rule of privilege. The rule with respect to privileges applies at all stages of all actions, cases, and proceedings.

(d) Rules inapplicable. The rules (other than with respect to privileges) do not apply in the following situations:

(1) Preliminary questions of fact. The determination of questions of fact preliminary to admissibility of evidence when the issue is to be determined by the court under rule 104.

(2) Grand jury. Proceedings before grand juries.

(3) Miscellaneous proceedings. Proceedings for extradition or rendition; preliminary examinations in criminal cases; sentencing, or granting or revoking probation; issuance of warrants for arrest, criminal summonses, and search warrants; and proceedings with respect to release on bail or otherwise.

(e) Rules applicable in part. In the following proceedings these rules apply to the extent that matters of evidence are not provided for in the statutes which govern procedure therein or in other rules prescribed by the Supreme Court pursuant to statutory authority: the trial of misdemeanors and other petty offenses by United States magistrate judges; review of agency actions when the facts are subject to trial de novo under section 706(2)(F) of title 5, United States Code; review of orders of the Secretary of Agriculture under section 2 of the Act entitled "An Act to authorize association of producers of agricultural products" approved February 18, 1922 (7 U.S.C. 292), and under sections 6 and 7(c) of the Perishable Agricultural Commodities Act, 1930 (7 U.S.C. 499f, 499g(c)); naturalization and revocation of naturalization under sections 310-318 of the Immigration and Nationality Act (8 U.S.C. 1421-1429); prize proceedings in admiralty under sections 7651-7681 of title 10, United States Code; review of orders of the Secretary of the Interior under section 2 of the Act entitled "An Act authorizing associations of producers of aquatic products" approved June 25, 1934 (15 U.S.C. 522); review of orders of petroleum control boards under section 5 of the Act entitled "An Act to regulate interstate and foreign commerce in petroleum and its products by prohibiting the shipment in such commerce of petroleum and its products produced in violation of State law, and for other purposes," approved February 22, 1935 (15 U.S.C. 715d); actions for fines, penalties, or forfeitures under part V of title IV of the Tariff Act of 1930 (19 U.S.C. 1581-1624), or under the Anti-Smuggling Act (19 U.S.C. 1701-1711); criminal libel for condemnation, exclusion of imports, or other proceedings under the Federal Food, Drug, and Cosmetic Act (21 U.S.C. 301-392); disputes between seamen under sections 4079, 4080, and 4081 of the Revised Statutes (22 U.S.C. 256-258); habeas corpus under sections 2241-2254 of title 28, United States Code; motions to vacate, set aside or correct sentence under section 2255 of title 28, United States Code; actions for penalties for refusal to transport destitute seamen under section 4578 of the Revised Statutes (46 U.S.C. 679); actions against the United States under the Act entitled "An Act authorizing suits against the United States in admiralty for damage caused by and salvage service rendered to public vessels belonging to the United States, and for other purposes," approved March 3, 1925 (46 U.S.C. 781-790), as implemented by section 7730 of title 10, United States Code.

Rule 1102 — Amendments

Amendments to the Federal Rules of Evidence may be made as provided in section 2072 of title 28 of the United States Code.

Rule 1103 — Title

These rules may be known and cited as the Federal Rules of Evidence.